the widowers' MANUAL

the widowers' MANUAL

Unrevealed Cornerstones to Regenerate Your Life

WOUTER LOOTEN

NEW YORK

the widowers' MANUAL
Unrevealed Cornerstones to Regenerate Your Life

ISBN: 978-1-61448-180-5 paperback
ISBN: 978-1-61448-181-2 eBook
Library of Congress Control Number: 2011944160

Morgan James Publishing
The Entrepreneurial Publisher
5 Penn Plaza, 23rd Floor
New York City, New York 10001
(212) 655-5470 office • (516) 908-4496 fax
www.MorganJamesPublishing.com

Cover Design by:
Rachel Lopez
www.r2cdesign.com

Interior Design by:
Bonnie Bushman
bonnie@caboodlegraphics.com

To absent friends

CONTENTS

I wake up. I had an awful dream.

I'm all sweaty. My heart is pounding in my chest.

I'm still scared and my head hurts.

I open my eyes and I look up at an unusual ceiling.

I recognize it though.

I'm in my parents' guest room.

Then it hits me.

It wasn't a dream.

I stare at the unused pillow beside me.

The confirmation is devastating.

She's not there.

INTRODUCTION

THE FIRST DAY OF THE rest of my life started on June 5th 1997. It was a Thursday. The day my world began as a blank page again. Unwritten. I didn't have a pen and I didn't have any ideas for a story line. I still didn't understand what had happened the day before. I was still wondering if it were true.

If people back then had showed me a future image of myself more than a decade later, feeling energetic, enthusiastic and truly enjoying life, I would not have believed them. My future had stopped yesterday. The day they told me my wife had been killed.

I wonder if you remember the last time when you were in a situation where you thought you could conquer the world? Can you look back at moments in time where you were so high on adrenaline that you felt you were invincible? In those moments everything just fell into place, and you thought, "This is what life is all about! I am on the top of the world." Wouldn't you wish all your days were filled with occasions, which give you feelings of immense power? Don't you agree in such moments you could easily handle whatever challenge to come across your path? Yet sometimes you run into confrontations, which are simply too colossal to manage. Sometimes you find yourself facing a challenge, which makes you want to give up as well. This time you feel like you have been defeated. It makes you want to throw in the towel.

Your wife died.

These words could sound pretty blank for all the non-widowers out there. However, if you have received the ticket to join our club, you'll find yourself within the most chaotic and surreal situation imaginable. To remember the time when you were conquering the world is not on the top of your mind anymore. The feeling that you are indestructible is not present.

Energy, vitality and joy changed into apathy and desolation. You are lost. There are no more words and thoughts. In your despair you look around like a kid with big wondering eyes, not understanding what the adults are doing, hoping that someone will tell you this is nothing but a bad dream. There is no more sense in the world. All logic and reason have disappeared from your life. You have the feeling of being in a cocoon. You are not able to think, to hear or to see clearly. You're alone in space where no one and nothing can reach you. You want life to be as it was before, but it just isn't. It's simply not possible. That world, that life, isn't there anymore. You understand that life goes on because you are still here and you see other people doing their everyday stuff, but you are basically functioning as a zombie. Without any effort you feed yourself instinctively. You couldn't care less for your job. You don't even care for life itself. However, it is absurd to find yourself in such a state. This is not you. This is not what you were set out to do. You had dreams, ideas and plans. You had projects that meant something to you, which were important to you. Yet, all at once they have totally lost their value.

Perhaps you didn't think of it constantly, but your wife was always part of your imagined future. And now she's gone? How is that even possible? What does this mean for you? What does this mean for your dreams? What does it signify for your future?

You're at a road's end, at least, that's what you think. That's how you feel. But is it really? Is this also your end of the line or could there be more? Would there be a possibility for a new beginning? Very unlikely you would say.

After public speaking, to die is the biggest fear we have in life. We don't like to think or talk about death. We are not taught how to deal with it. The lack of knowledge makes us scared of death and therefore we neglect the subject. This works remarkably well for as long as we actually don't have to deal with it. Then again, we are not completely ignorant. Although we don't know what it is exactly, we do know that it is the end of our lives. But then what? Is there still something beyond death? Some of us believe in a heaven or in an afterlife, others don't. In any case, we don't have hard evidence, which would establish the fact of any form of continuation after we die. So we simply say, "If you don't have proof, it doesn't exist", end of discussion. Now, we can skip to speak in public, yet everybody is going to face death sooner or later. When we must, we are not prepared to deal with it. It blows us away, especially when it happens to someone very close to us. Especially when it happens sooner.

In my case I didn't really have a problem with speaking in public. As a matter of fact, I have always enjoyed it. Instead, general fear number two hit me. Obviously not directly, but the destructive impact was total nonetheless. My wife died when she was only twenty-six years old. It completely knocked me off my feet. I didn't know how to cope with the emotions and I was dysfunctional in society for a long time. Certainly, I was physically present: I worked and I went on doing things somehow, but I was totally disoriented. Completely out of focus. Moving around like a ship without a rudder.

STRUGGLE

This book tells my tale. It describes the path I took as a twenty-nine year old guy from the minute I learned I had lost my spouse, to where I am today. With your indulgence I will show you exactly how I found reason and purpose to go on, starting from a similar condition as you are in right now. I know how hard it is for you at this moment. After years and years of breaking my back and hitting a lot of walls in my effort to move forward, I finally sorted out a course of action, which has led me toward a resourceful state of mind and the resulting outcome in my life. Today I find myself living life to the fullest and enjoying every day of it. I now understand it is possible to continue to live with energy and passion. I developed a way where the pain of the loss goes hand in hand with the energy and curiosity of living today and tomorrow. Of course this is possible also for you! I am pleased to share the outline of how to achieve this with you in the upcoming pages. In this way, you don't have to battle for more than a decade in order to figure a way out for yourself. Of course you have to take action. I don't hand you a pill as if you would be having a headache. It won't be a stroll in the park. This is hard work. Then again I believe it should be hard work. The harder it is, the more valuable your relationship with your wife was. The more love you felt, the more devastated you are now. The personification of that love has been taken away from you, and that is exactly why you feel like you have been ripped apart. That's why nothing makes sense anymore. You are shattered and you do not see how in the world you could go on living your life, but you can and you will if you want to.

This comprehensive book lays out practically where you are now, where you could go, how to do that and the impact your actions (and non-actions) have on you and your world. I am dedicated to help you here. I wish I had a book like this when I took the decision to start and rebuild my life. It would have saved me a lot of years of darkness. Years that I could I have spent preciously enjoying the memory of my wife while heading toward a new future. I didn't forget nor am I faking that nothing ever happened. I cherish the memories of my wife dearly. In effect, they help me immensely in creating new steps I take on my way to bringing my new dream alive.

A BOOK FOR GUYS

When I started to write this book I thought of composing a set of practical tools that would offer you a way out of this mess. I wanted to write a book for guys. Practical guys, who don't just need a narrative about how tough it is after your girl dies and wonder if you could ever overcome the dreadful pain. Of course it sucks that your wife died and of course it hurts, but what are you going to do about it? It's done! Let's get a grip and move on.

Now just stop there for a moment. Obviously there's much more to it. Let's not cut corners here!

In general it's true that men are expected to be tough. They're certainly not weak and in any given situation they quickly pick up where they left off. Besides, money talks so it's essential to get back to work as soon as possible! Yet, you're facing quite a challenge here. In this case you just do not have the ability to get your act together. There's no more structure and you've lost the overview.

Therefore, in effect, I thought some more of whom I wanted to reach here. Who are the ones that are supposed to read my book? I realized that for me it has been a while since my wife died. I have been dealing with this stuff for almost a decade and a half.

If you're new, you are still in the first part of some vertical loop of the roller coaster called "The Widower's Life", not knowing what is up and down. I'm already in the flat part.

Then there are the guys who have lost their spouse already some years ago and they have tried to pick up their lives as well as they could, but somehow they just don't seem to manage to get a grip. They kind of went on with their lives and they ask themselves when things will finally be better. Yet without work, results don't come. Time alone won't heal this wound. If you want to build a new and fulfilling life, you need good and reliable tools to get the job done right!

So I changed my approach. I wanted to reach both groups, the rookies and the veterans, and fulfill a need as well as I could. The best thing of course, would be to describe a way in which your wife would return to you, and I truly wish I could that for you. I wish I could reset the clock. Unfortunately and obviously, I have to settle for the next best thing: I will teach the guidelines on how you, as a widower, can create a rich and full life.

If you are interested to find out how to put the experience of becoming a widower into perspective in a way that gives you the ability to create order from chaos, read this book. If you are tired of being stuck and you want to know how you can develop yourself to get back on track so you will have an active life where you are fully present, read this book. If you want to know how you can use this experience as leverage in order to even rise above your current self, read this book. It is not your everyday book on how you could overcome your spouse's demise. It doesn't give you an answer why she went away. Importantly, it gives you an outline of what you can do now.

TACTICS

To do so I will present you a set of five guideposts, called the "Widowers' Manual Anchors", which I developed and used to get back on track and it changed my life. I will show you how I've dealt with the pain. I'll teach you how important it is to share your story with the world. I will talk about letting go and what you can do when you meet new people in your life. Finally I'll teach you the importance of caring, and although I know that's one of the problems right now, because you probably just don't care anymore, it is the one element that will pull you through this whole ordeal.

This is the one book that shows you clarity in how you can cope with the death of your wife and what you can do to deal with this devastating situation powerfully. You can do this with eagerness, excitement and the everlasting love you have for your

xviii   *the* widowers' MANUAL

spouse. She knows who you are and how you are. So she will expect from whatever place she is right now, for you to show life that it cannot mess with you. Without conceiving where you are, and knowing what to do to get out of this mayhem, you will stay stuck. You will not be able to live your life. Negative emotions like fear, hesitation and feelings of wondering if you can do this, are erased by education. Informing yourself about the how-to will clear your doubts.

I therefore encourage you to read the whole book. Perhaps there will be passages that you want to skip or scan quickly. Most likely you won't put the given advice into play all together at once. But read it all now, because as Brendon Burchard puts it, "The time to have the map is before you enter the woods." You are heading into a new direction and you don't know the way yet. How would you know which is the "right" way if you wouldn't recognize the "wrong" way. You catch my drift? You don't have to apply all the information present in the book this instant. However, I want you to be aware of what's available. Therefore, when you decide to go out there, you have a storage bin full of information to go to, anytime you wish. I just want you to know how all of these things work. So when you do decide to hit the ground running, you have the background and the perspective of the different ways you could head for.

The Widowers' Manual offers you the knowledge needed to give you the reassurance to get going. Once you're on the road, you'll learn the real game so you can win it. To overcome the death of your spouse is not about analyzing where you were, it's about deciding where you want to go, and beyond. That's what this book is about.

PERSONAL NOTE

Although I mainly use the words "wife" and "spouse" in this book, I don't distinguish any difference between men who are and who aren't married by law. I was married, but the contractual marriage didn't define my state of being. This book is for all guys out there who have lost their wife, girlfriend or partner.

I know that, in spite of what has happened, deep down inside of you there still is the old you; the one that dreams; the one that wants to make something out of your life. The one you need to get back on track so you can create the life you want, and need for yourself. It is my mission to help you find that person. I'd therefore advise you to see this book as a workbook. Get involved, answer the questions, and put things into play, because once the storm wears off, you'll start to see the first signs of a new future.

Wouter

Chapter 1

THE SPORTS ILLUSTRATED COVER GIRL

"AND THEY LIVED HAPPILY ever after." We have been hearing this particular phrase at the end of so many stories for as long as we can remember. We love this sentence. We love it because we know it, it's familiar, and it is how a story *should* end. Therefore as a young adult, I logically pursued my own great story that of course had to lead to a wonderful and happy ending. What did I need for that? Well, obviously some money, my health, an education and of course the girl. So off I went. I started organizing these basic elements for a happy life. In today's instant-satisfaction world it is not that difficult to get what you want. You just go out there and choose from a large variety of options. As a result, within a short period of time, I found myself with everything that I required: a job, a house, a car and a wife. Now I was settled. But then something happened I did not foresee, something unknown to me. Something occurred that left me speechless, desperate, confused and infuriated. Something that caused pain, so much pain!

My wife died.

I didn't understand. She was out of the country on a business trip and I just spoke to her on the phone the day before yesterday. Everything was fine. So how could this be? Maybe it's a mix-up? Were these people for real? What were they saying? This couldn't be true!

But it was. My ultimate nightmare had become reality. I could not believe it. I was devastated. I felt like an empty shell; my spirit had been torn out of me. I felt defeated by life and I was angry as hell. I didn't know what to do or where to go, but then again, I didn't give a damn. The world didn't make sense anymore. This was not supposed to happen. We were supposed to grow old together. We were presumed to sit in a rocking chair on the porch outside our home, watching our grand children play. Why did this happen? Why did I lose her? What was I supposed to do now? What was the meaning of all this? How could I go on? Would I even go on, and for what? Give me a reason! But no one could give me one.

WE MEET AND WE SEPARATE

She was eighteen when we met, I was twenty-one. It was spring. She had long dark blond hair and the body of a Sports Illustrated cover girl. I instantly fell in love with her. We went to the same business school. After four years of hard work we both graduated and two years later I asked her dad if I could marry his daughter. A short time after that we bought our first little house: a little cottage in the countryside. We were very happy. We both had jobs and a bright future ahead of us. One day in June however, just out of nowhere, this all changed dramatically.

I remember sitting at my desk at work. My office viewed the entrance of our building. Suddenly I saw a familiar car driving up the parking lot. I recognized the car. It was my wife's colleague. Do you know the feeling when you see someone familiar but the person and the place don't correlate? There's something strange about the picture. Well, this was such a moment. I knew my wife's colleague, but his office was a two hours drive away. So what in the heck was he doing here? Actually, I didn't even allow myself the time to ask that question. The feeling, almost the confirmation, of something being terribly wrong was already choking me. Without saying a word to anybody I stood up, walked out of the office and down to the reception. We met each other in the hallway. He looked at me and without any introduction he spoke the three most destructive words I have ever heard in my life,

"Judith is dead."

I received news that my wife had been killed on a business trip in the Far East. At the time she was working for a garden decoration distributor and she had just started to design some pottery. Because she had put in a lot of effort, she was granted permission to go and visit the factories in Vietnam in order to see the first production rolling out of the ovens. It was a great success. I remember she called me on Monday night to tell me enthusiastically that she and her two colleagues had been working really hard and as a small treat to themselves they would take a couple of hours off in order to visit the local market on Wednesday morning. The plane back home would be the next day. She never made it onto that plane.

This particular morning she was visiting the different booths of a well-known tourist market in Vietnam's capital Ho Chi Minh City, formerly known as Saigon. Suddenly and totally out of the blue, some crazy lunatic ran up to her and just stabbed her in the middle of this street market full of people. The long, narrow knife pierced her heart. It went precisely in between two ribs and caused cardiac trauma. I mean, what are the chances of that happening? She died that day far away from her family, her friends and me. My world was gone, destroyed. There was just ... nothing. I went into a blur for several days. I guess it's some kind of a self-preservation mechanism of the mind in order to protect your heart from actually breaking. Nevertheless, it felt like a hand was squeezing it; pure heartache.

I was twenty-nine years old and a widower.

The days and months that followed I went on automatic pilot. I ate because someone put food in front of me. I went to sleep because everyone else had gone to bed so why bother to stick around? I didn't care about anything, especially about life. I got drunk in bars and was a pain in the ass for the people close to me. I was in a destructive mood. I didn't want to live anymore, but I still kept on going somehow. I guessed there was something to live for after all, but what? This was my buddy I lost here, my best friend and the love of my life! I would never find someone like her again, not ever! This was not the dream I had projected. I wanted to live my life with Judith. I wanted to enjoy the house we had bought just six months before. We had still so many plans, and now the foundation of those aspirations was gone. *We* were gone. I fell in a deep dark hole.

I AM A WIDOWER

This is the story I have learned to share with the world. However, the first years I barely even talked about the event. I only shared my stories and emotions with my closest friends. They didn't require clear explanations from me because they understood that I was a mess. For them it was a clear picture that my head and thoughts were in disarray because this whole story just didn't make sense at all.

We all search for the meaning of life. But what meaning can you give to it, the moment one of life's most profound experiences crosses your path: the death of your partner. You are confronted with destruction when you've only just started to build. Suddenly you have been labeled "Widower", and you have absolutely no clue how to respond to that. It is surreal. It is staggering. What in the world is happening? The word widower gives you a strange sensation. A widower is usually an older guy who has lived a long life with his spouse and at the end, one of the two goes first. Unfortunately for him, she has the first ticket, but not before she's at least eighty! We see a widower as a poor old guy who stares at nothing on a bench in the park or who silently plays cards in a cafe with some mates who also have lost their wives. He makes sure his house is one hundred percent neat and he always looks at you with those sad, hollow eyes. As if someone took away his spirit before his time is actually up. Just waiting to join his wife on the other side. And now you are one too?

"Time flies when you're having fun", people say, and I guess that's true. In our case you could easily say, "When you become a widower, time stops." It's a freeze frame, which just allows you to look back. There's only the past tense. You have to start talking when the two of you "were", and when she "did" that cute performance and "do you remember when".

Time is important to people, as it is scarce. We have only so much of it. So you try to fit in as many activities as possible. Our lives are totally controlled by our agenda's and schedules. Not just at work, but also during the weekends and even on holidays. As kids we don't realize this: we don't worry about time and we just model the grownups. This changes when you've turned twenty-five. Then you start to measure time in periods: age landmarks. It's a big deal when you turn thirty as you have to start to show some responsibility and when you hit the big 4-0 your life is practically over. Then you have your family years until you retire at sixty-five, subsequently eat eggnog at Christmas, look at the pictures of your grand children and then the light goes out. This would be a nutshell scenario for someone's life. But what if the screenplay was a bit different? What if you don't reach the part of looking at your grandkids' photos? What about if life decides that it gets dark when she's still much too young? What if *she* just happens to be your wife? What do you do then? You're not trained for that. You are not prepared for that. You and the people around you are not ready for that, but you have to be. You don't have a choice.

If we look at life expectancy, the statistical expected number of years of life remaining at a given age, we see that in the western world the average age of death is seventy-eight years for men and eighty-two for women. But these figures don't apply to you! You wish they did! Yet here you are and you just learned that your wife died. Your world is scattered to pieces. Life literary knocked you down. Of course you're not thinking about death when you're thirty. You didn't anticipate this! You desperately try to get a grip on the situation, but you're not able to. Not by far. Frantically you look around you. People are talking to you, but you don't hear a thing. It's like your head is in a bell jar. Reason does not exist anymore. Answers do not exist anymore. There are just questions. Why? What? How?

In effect, I tried to pick up somehow where I had left off, but quickly I realized that to deal with the emotions was too much for me to bear alone.

Elisabeth Kübler-Ross, a Swiss-American psychiatrist, wrote about the five stages of grief, which are denial, anger, bargaining, depression, and acceptance. In general, people experience most of these stages, though in no particular order, after being faced with the reality of death. Needless to say Mrs. Kübler-Ross has done some great work, but how do you actually integrate this theory in real life? To answer that I thought it might be a good idea to seek some external help.

A couple of weeks after Judith died I went to see a psychiatrist, but after about ten minutes we both decided that this was not the path for me. I am a guy and guys look for solutions. Men want practical solutions for problems. I had lost my wife and the only solution would be, to get her back. Plain and simple. "So Mister Psychiatrist, what do you have to say about that?" Poor guy. Not one of my best days and surely not one of my friendliest approaches, but I guess he got the picture. I'm not saying to avoid seeking professional help. Skilled aid is very valuable, especially in the long run. However, in my case I was hurting so much, that I needed instant results. I required practical ways to get rid of the pain, and this psychiatrist could not provide what I wanted. I don't do drugs and so I realized that I just had to stand the pain. But how was I supposed to do that? This was not like a light crash with my motorbike. My goodness, someone just ripped my heart out! How do you stand such pain?

In order to accept it, I understood that I had to be calmer first, but I wasn't. On the contrary! I was freaking out in order to find some form of reason. In fact, what I was trying to do is to search for the meaning of life: did our relationship matter? Did I matter? Do I still matter? Later on I conceived that to connect pain with love could be a very healthy approach. I was able to reduce the pain by focusing on the love itself. That worked remarkably well.

To distract myself I went on trips. I went to New York. I wandered around in Central Park and I visited the places where New Yorkers would be. I wanted to be one of the "normal" people, and I wanted to experience reality. I didn't want to be in an absurd, preposterous situation like being a twenty-nine year old widower! I wanted to feel alive! I also went rock climbing in the French Alps, and I remember being extremely scared at three hundred feet up, hanging like Spiderman on a cliff. I recall cursing everything and everybody at the time due to my fear, but I also felt the adrenaline pumping. I bought a new motorcycle and made a tour throughout Europe. I went to Mallorca and I laid on the beach in Cancun, Mexico. I was a world traveller. Something everybody wants to do, and I did it! And I felt miserable all the time, but I thought that as long as I kept myself busy I didn't have to face the fact that I already had to burry my wife. So I kept on running like a chicken with its head cut off, and in the process, I was certain to have the back up from my friends. But then I had a strange experience.

I AM YOUR WIDOWER

Something occurred to me that hadn't happened before. Together with some friends I went on a weekend trip. This was about a year after my wife had died. During the day we gathered and we left for this vacation home we had rented for a couple of days. It was good to see my friends all together. Well, not "all" of course: one seat was empty. At night we went out to a bar and as usual I did what I used to do in bars back in those days: I got drunk and I acted like a moron. The next day I noticed some grumpy faces. At first I thought it was due to their hangovers, but then I felt disapproval and even anger toward me. I didn't get the picture at first, but then someone made a remark from which I understood that some of my friends were mad at me for my behavior the previous night at the bar. However, this coming from my friends hit a wrong note on my keypad and off we were, being angry at each other. Bitterly I left the house and went for a walk on the beach. I didn't understand the reaction of these people and I was aggravated that they didn't support me. How was it possible that they did not feel for me? Did they not get what I went through? What I was still going through? Later on I understood that my friends intended to use that weekend as a kind of memorial for Judith. They wanted to remember her, honor her and have an almost spiritual get together. I on the other hand, was already doing so every day. Each day I thought about her, remembering our times together and looking up at the sky at night hoping to see some star sparkling as if to tell me, "I'm okay up here!" So to go out with my mates on a weekend trip was a distraction for me. I finally had some days off! I didn't have to cope with the loss for a little while!

Evidently, we started out on different levels. Though everybody was trying to look for some sense in this clutter, we all started from our own experiences and opinions on how a deceased loved one should be commemorated. Each and every one of us had begun his or her search within a different reality realm. The problem was that all of us wanted to find the answer within the boundaries of our own mental world. This is what caused the clash: when you search for reality, what reality are you talking about? Is it real to have a wife, or is it real to have lost her? Should you remember her by organizing an emotional setting with candles, or should you party until you drop for one evening because you feel the need to live life that way? What are you supposed to do?

WHO AM I?

So I learned that things had changed. Rules had shifted. I realized I was not only a widower in my life, but also a widower in other people's lives. And as a widower you have to keep up a certain appearance. You are supposed to mourn in a specific way. Not in my way, but in the other people's way. Boy, did I fail there. Of course I failed. You ask one hundred people the question, "How do you mourn?" and you get a hundred different answers. So when are you doing the right thing? Never! Tossing and turning I had been racking my brain about the different opinions of the people around me and those of my own. It has caused a lot of problems for me. I didn't know what to do. It was not my intention to hurt anybody's feelings, yet with her death also my identity that I had wrapped around us being a couple had gone lost. I had not only lost her, I also had lost myself.

On top of that I now was labeled "Widower", but I wasn't taught how to be a widower. I didn't want to be one in the first place, and to find a way to create a mix of being simultaneously angry, sad and respectful was too difficult. It was too much for me. How was I supposed to get out of this emotional trap?

Then I thought of this metaphor: as the flight attendants in an airplane tell you at the start of each flight, "In case the cabin pressure fails and the oxygen masks appear, first put on your own mask, then help others." I therefore decided to help myself first and try to be as respectful as I could to others in the process.

TRYING TO PICK UP AGAIN

After this I went to work. Not my old job, but a new one. I started as an account manager. Not a great choice. To be on the road all day and lots of times alone in the car didn't help me to get ahead. It made me feel even more lonely and miserable. One time I even had to stop the car because tears blinded me. I was a mess.

A short time after that I bought a new apartment. It was a beautiful place in the center of a town close to the nightlife. In this way at least I would not feel alone! My family and friends helped me moving and were all very enthusiastic about my new home. They were trying to lift up my spirits, but I didn't care much about the place. Later that same day one of my best friends, Max, entered the apartment. He owned an electronics store and he had sold me a new TV. He came through the doorway with this huge cardboard box and saw me standing completely lost in the middle of all the fuss. He put aside the television and he said something simple that changed everything, "Come on, let's go and have a beer." Max understood perfectly what I needed at that moment. I needed personal attention. I just wanted a true friend that sits next to me in a bar while having a beer. No fancy apartment could beat that! So it became clear to me that in order to find a way out, I needed genuine people who were just *there* for me. At the same time I wondered, "Why Max?" I mean, the rest of my friends and family were also sincere people who wanted to help me. Well, Max had also suffered loss in his life and I related to that. As I mentioned earlier, the knowledge of not having to talk about the loss, not to have to explain what I felt, gave me peace. However, just to have people being *there* didn't do the whole trick for me. Of course it was a start, but I knew that in order to make any progress in my situation, I had to take action, and so I did. Step by step I got back on track. At some point in time I found a new girl with whom now I'm happily married. We have a little girl and I wouldn't want to miss her for the world. It has been a long, bumpy and steep road. The tar isn't impeccable yet. Still it is heading in the direction I chose for myself and I know that with every step I take, the road becomes smoother.

NOT THE END OF MY LIFE

So I guess I made it back, but looking over my shoulder I have made some big mistakes in the process. I could have been where I am today a lot sooner. I have missed precious time that I would not have missed if I had known the things then that I know today.

In these years the feeling inside of me that I should do something with the knowledge that this experience had brought me grew stronger and stronger. By becoming a widower, my vision on how I could and even how I should live my life had been transformed. My views on life and how I saw my role in it had changed.

My perspective on what was important in the world had altered and I wanted to share these ideas. Yet I didn't have the words straight. My feelings and emotions were still overwhelming. I couldn't describe exactly what I wanted to say. This was caused by the fact that I didn't know *how* to share my story and my views, and so I went looking for techniques, which could help me to pinpoint my ideas.

Let's take a look at my approach on how I got clarity in sharing my story. I figured out a way in my search for a solution by deciding that first of all this was not the end of my life. Although I was totally heartbroken, destroyed and destructive, I told myself not to quit. This would be the beginning of a new life. As I wanted to know how I could build a new future for myself, I wanted to know what possibilities I had and how well I could actually operate in my situation within our society. In other words: how damaged was I? I decided to study the confinement of my self-esteem, and therefore I started to search my limits. I became reckless at times and extremely thoughtful at others. I took on adventurous challenges, hid myself away from the world from time to time, and implemented my search geographically. In the past ten years I have moved around and lived in different countries throughout Europe. I told myself that I could perhaps find clarity in other cultures and in other environments. Of course I was just trying to outrun the ghosts I had created for myself, but I didn't realize that at the time. Certainly I would not fix my problem by changing my location every couple of years as one crucial element in my baggage always stayed the same: me! I always dragged myself along.

As long as I didn't work on myself by looking inside of me and distinguishing the facts, which were really important to me, I would keep on moving. And that's exactly what I did.

It all started when I met an Italian girl in Paris. I always loved anything Italian and therefore I took the opportunity when it presented itself by introducing myself to this girl, a lovely young woman from Turin. She lived in the French capital at the time, but after two months of going back and forth between Paris and Holland, I could persuade her to come and live with me in the Netherlands. Not long after she had moved in with me, I proposed to her. We got married in Las Vegas, just the two of us. Although it was really fun, in retrospect I guess I would have preferred to have at least our parents present at the ceremony. Now they were watching the scene on the Internet shot by the webcam in the chapel. The whole six minutes forty of it. Anyway, looking back is easy, so I don't bother to worry about it. We decided to do it our way at the time, and so we did. After our honeymoon to Bora Bora we came back to Holland, where we stayed for a while. There she got pregnant. However, to be in a country where she hardly spoke the language while expecting a baby wasn't very appealing to my new wife. She longed for her family, and so we decided to move to Turin, Italy. Four months later our beautiful baby girl was born. I was very proud and I thought that I had finally found my peace and quiet. I was a father and I had to handle my responsibilities. I went searching for a job, but without having sorted out what was important to me, this didn't work out very well. The mistake again was to think that my environment would help me create the new me I wanted to be.

FLYING DUTCHMAN

Then an opportunity in Spain came along. I sold this idea to my new wife, and off we went, but Spain didn't do the trick for me either. Certainly the place was nice, but after a couple of months even the view on the Mediterranean Sea isn't that special anymore. So we moved back to Holland to a steady job, a house, a garden and a car. Finally a normal family! Some years later however, I found myself wrestling with the same issues again. Still I felt restless, and I had difficulty focusing on my job. I was wondering why it was so important to target an even higher turnover for the company I was working for, and I still didn't see the higher purpose in life. I was always waiting for someone to present the answer to me. Besides that, my wife could not get used to Holland, found a job in Paris, France and I used that as an excuse for my next move to another country. In the meantime our relationship was not going well. We were exhausted from moving around. The stress of our nomad existence and the fact that I constantly put my faith in others for me to feel better was taking its toll. Paris would not offer an exception either. I felt we were growing apart. Five years later, my wife was offered a new position in Florence, Italy and she wanted to take that opportunity. I didn't want to let go of our little family and so we started to pack our stuff again.

Meanwhile, over the years, piece by piece, it had become clearer to me that the answers I was seeking, were in fact not to be found "somewhere". My problems were all stashed up inside of me. The ghosts I had been trying to outrun were still there. I truly felt like the Flying Dutchman: I was never going to make port as long as I did not study myself and find clarity about my dreams and aspirations.

No peaceful harbor would grant me a spot until I had sorted out what I expected from life. My ghosts would keep on haunting me. In fact they were smiling down at me.

To get rid of them, the only solution would be to start working on my inner self and consequently be able to create a fulfilling life myself. No one else could do that for me.

SOUL SEARCHING

So along the way I slowly realized the misunderstanding. Instead of observing the outside world, I began to look at what was happening, on the inside. I went soul searching. I aimed my focus on what principles I identified myself with. What values were important to me? Once I had my values sorted out, I started to test them, and again I found out through trial and error what was good for me and what didn't work out that well. The most important thing I discovered was that you can think about ideas or activities as long as you want; yet it is action that defines the outcome. Perhaps a no-brainer, I grant you, but very true nevertheless. How many times do you think of doing something and yet you don't act upon it? So if you want to grow, take action. If you want to change your situation, take action. If you really want to live your life, take action. The best way to learn new things is simply by doing them. At first you might fail, but once you get the hang of it, your results start to show.

A CLEAR VISION

You are in a similar position now. You understand that the situation is irreversible. To avoid the pain is not a possibility. The pain is not going to go away. It is here to stay. Another alternative is hard to get. You feel the extremely urgent need to have your spouse back, but this is unobtainable. The idea of not seeing her anymore drives you crazy. Of course you have your memories, photos and maybe some videos, but that's not going to do it for you. The thought alone of not to have her in your life anymore hurts beyond words. It is therefore necessary to find a way to deal with this agony because you are still you! Although you have been beaten up and you are tremendously hurt, your core is still there. You still want to enjoy and pursue the nice things and activities in life. You still have your dreams. Of course they will be different, and perhaps you will now go after your dreams from a different perspective, but eventually you still are going to pursue what you were set out to do: to live your life. This will require effort, intelligence and insights. But most of all, you'll need to be clear on the reason why and how you will fight your way back. And even though you might question whether or not you actually will live your life again, I can tell you that you will! You are determined to do just that. You've picked up this book! A first step has been taken. That says enough about your conviction.

This experience gives you an opportunity to grow. I'm not talking about the fact that you've lost your wife. That's painful beyond imagination. No, I'm referring to the experience, the story of loss and the fact that in spite of this tremendous pain, both emotionally and physically, you're still here, because you've made the choice to be here.

Your choice regarding your future can basically take you in two directions: up or down, you can win or lose the game called "Life".

When you lose, you become dark. You will see everything negatively. You'll be careless and without ambition. You're not interested in doing good or in making a difference.

Or you can win. In this case, you'll be grateful to be part of the world. You understand how delicate life is, how much you can do and the importance to celebrate it every day. You get how definitive it can be, but you also know how strong and resilient you are. You have lived through this. You can move mountains. You could figure out a way to exit this mess. You can develop a clear vision on where you want to go and what you want to do. In this way you have clarity and clarity is power. But know this: it won't get better overnight. You have to understand that you have to put in a lot of effort and time. If you want to create the foundation for a great new life, you will have to work hard for it. Stay focused in this process.

People try to manage so much complexity that one forgets it's the simple things in life that often make the difference in the world. But nowadays we are so incredibly busy trying to do everything at the same time, that we often miss the few things that really matter.

If you don't focus, the possibility exists that while trying to organize everything, you don't get anything done in the end. So in order to tackle this, the answer is: get a clear vision of where you want to go, keep that in mind and then start to work really hard to get there!

Chapter 2

A CRASH COURSE
IN HOW TO BE A
WIDOWER

I HAVE ALWAYS BEEN interested in the area of personal development. I'm a curious guy. I like to learn and I like to grow as a person. I love to educate myself because I feel very strongly about having control over my own destiny. I believe that the more I understand my mental and physical state, the better I can manage specific situations or circumstances. Therefore I have been studying the big names in this specific industry for over the past fifteen years. I have been following people like for example Tony Robbins, Debbie Ford and Wayne Dyer. My interest in this field rose after my wife passed away. Apparently I felt like I did not have control anymore and that scared me. So I increased the number of books I read, did online courses, went to see psychologists, gurus, life coaches, and attended multiple seminars about personal growth and human behavior. I am still doing that today. As a widower aiming to rebuild his future, I thought of how I could use the information I gained throughout these years in a way that would serve me the best. In addition I talked more about the theories I learned and the experiences I had with the people around me. I truly believe we have to keep on educating ourselves. Education is the source of growth and evolution in our lives. I also feel that we are responsible for the quality of our world. So I understood that if I would share my knowledge with others, taking myself as an example, I could help increase the quality of these people's lives. Simply because of the fact that they are part of my world, their higher level of well being, would surely spin off on my level of well being. Moreover, the feedback I got, was valuable information for my learning curve. A win-win situation: both my audience and I would take advantage. In effect, I was so thrilled about this idea that I decided to make it my life's work, and so I packed up all the information, knowledge and experiences that I gained over the years, integrated these facts with my expertise as a widower and I put it all in this book.

To get started I used three simple steps to sort things out: *wake up, get up and start moving.*

First of all you need to wake up and be aware of where you are. What is your current condition and how did you get there in the first place. Now this seems obvious, but there's a little more to it. Just stick with me for a while.

Secondly, it is necessary to get up before you can start to move again. In order to rise and shine quickly and fully, it is important to understand how much influence you have on yourself. What are your choices of action? If you're focused on creating a livable life, you have to find out what is valuable to you. What are the essential ingredients to live your life the way you want to? Once you know that, you get ready to take the necessary steps in order to achieve your life's mission.

The third step is about starting to move in the direction you have set out for yourself and re-create your life. How can you anchor yourself solidly into the ground allowing you to realize your new dream?

§ 2.1 WAKE UP

In this first step I would like to point out the difference between facts and stories.

One day some years ago, I attended a seminar about personal growth. We were discussing how a fact is different from a story. There was a woman in the room who had been having difficulties in keeping personal relationships. What happened to her? When she was nine years old she experienced her mother being drunk day in and day out, and while being intoxicated, her mom used to beat her up pretty badly. Nevertheless, this was her mom! She was supposed to love and to trust her. Yet, every day the little girl was afraid of getting smacked by her own mother. In order to make sense out of this absurd situation, she tried to find a logical explanation. That would be that people in close personal relationships hurt each other. Since you always want to back up your own beliefs, this "logical" reason became a truth for this woman. A fact, "In personal relationships you'll get hurt!" This was clearly a survivor's tactic, which helped her getting through a long painful period. It's not a powerful and energetic way to live your life, but we are not here to judge others, especially not nine year old kids. Years later, at the age of thirty-five, she found that she longed for a close relationship with somebody. Unfortunately, she was not able to establish one. She still did not confide in other people.

This was the story she shared with the rest of us. Then a remarkable thing happened. The seminar leader asked her one simple question, "Do you have a car?" Do I have a car? What is that supposed to mean? I'm having trouble in order to have deep meaningful relationships and you ask me if I own a car!? She replied, "Yeah, sure I have a car, so?" The trainer responded, "Would you give your car keys to a nine year old and let her drive your car?" Answer, "No of course not, are you crazy!" The seminar leader looked at her with a big disarming smile and quietly said, "So why would you let a nine year old child run your life?"

A big jaw-dropping silence.

FACTS & STORIES

Not only the woman, but also everybody else in the seminar understood the silly question about having a car. The decision the woman took twenty-six years ago was still controlling her life! The little girl inside of her did not grow up regarding relationships. Her "rule" was still blocking her.

Now, it's not enough to understand the Laws of Behavior. If you want to change something you have to choose to change it and take action, but it starts with awareness. First of all know this: there is a difference between a fact and a story. A fact is an actual event or circumstance. It has happened in the past and you don't have any influence on it. A story on the other end is a narrative, either true or fictitious, designed to interest, amuse, or instruct the hearer or reader. A story is often being made up and therefore you have influence on your story. You can change it, wherever and whenever! In the example above, the woman got beaten as a child: fact. Then she made up a story, "In personal relationships you get beaten up, so you cannot trust people." However, she could have created a totally different story. For example, "When people are drunk they can be violent, so it's better to stay out of the way!" With that information she might have been able to find a man, a sober one, and to have a loving relationship.

Do you see how strong a story works in your mind?

Your wife is no longer on this planet. That's a fact. But what you do with that information in terms of creating your story is totally up to you! You have that power. Perhaps you feel your current pain because you have a certain rule about the felicity your wife brought you in terms of time. Maybe you have decided that the happiness you experience in your life is to be measured in time. Somewhere along the road you have adopted or invented a story that if the two of you would live to be eighty, things would be all right. This rule was broken much too soon! But what if you decide to change that rule, that story? Instead of calculating a number of years, what if you decided that the bliss of the time together with your spouse was measured in terms of love and feelings of deep connection? Would it be more acceptable that's she's gone then, or do you think you could have loved her more? Would you have been able to create an even deeper connection? I'm not saying that's not possible, but I think it's important to understand that there are ways of alternative thinking. I believe it's good to question life's facts, assumptions and rules. It opens up your mind in order to notice that there are other paths in front of you that you could take. Whether you do that or not is your choice obviously. By the way, please notice that I describe the fact that your wife's gone in terms of *more acceptable*. I know you won't totally accept this. You never will. I know I haven't accepted it after more than ten years. I sometimes still get angry that life has pulled a stunt on me like this, but knowing I can change my rules and my stories whenever I want to, makes me feel powerful and gives me peace. It makes me aware of the fact that I have choice and therefore control over my life, and control is want we want.

Be aware that you're down. Life has knocked you down. It's like laying flat on your back in a boxing ring looking up to Mike Tyson who just smacked you in the head. Your vision is quite blurry to say the least. Any decision you would make in this state will not be as constructive as the one you'd make when you're fully conscious. Not only your world looks all foggy when you're on your back like this, but everything around you looks bigger and more overwhelming. It is very difficult to move forward lying dizzy, face up. You can try for as long as you want and think that your willpower does the job, but it won't. Not if you compare it with rising yourself up and starting to practice in getting ahead.

It is essential to understand where you are and how you are in order to change your situation. The next step would be to get up on your feet, stand straight and look at the world from a different perspective.

§ 2.2 GET UP

Once I was told that where your attention goes, the energy flows. I agree with that. Center on positive concepts and you will notice the universe providing you with just that. Focus on negativity and that's what you're going to encounter.

It's very dangerous to think, "My life is over" and, "I am never going to get over the death of my wife." The little voice in your head is having a ball when it can tell you, "I've told you so." So it is set, consciously and subconsciously, to search for situations, places and people that confirm it is all right to feel sad and depressed. Accordingly you actually end up feeling miserable, forlorn and staying right there in your dark spot on earth. On the other hand, to accept the pain for what it is and to decide that it will not stop you from living your life shows destiny that it cannot mess with you.

Understand that what you think is extremely important. Your thoughts will feed your feelings, which push you toward some kind of action, and of course your actions will result in a certain outcome.

So simply think for example, "How can I develop a rich and fulfilling life?" and, "How can I make today a great day?" This will make you head in a positive direction in which you will dig deep into your resources to come up with strong answers to these questions that gives you the capability to feel and to act powerfully. Your actions will then result in the success you're aiming for. The clearer you picture your result, the bigger the chance that you will achieve it. Imagine how, where and when you want to be. Then try to actually act how you would be in that situation. This will seem very strange to you, but it will become more natural when you practice it for a longer period. As with everything you rehearse, after a while it will become a normal conditioned pattern of your daily behavior.

If this is your mindset, you will find yourself on a very resourceful path bringing you lots of new opportunities. Yes, your mind will still play tricks on you for your own protection. It will scream out that you're behaving ridiculously, but guess what? You are not your mind; your mind is in fact mostly a gathering of other people's opinions. It's a cabinet folder filled with the experiences of others. Your family, friends and colleagues have provided you with their knowledge and experiences and you have stored that know-how in your head, but this knowledge is colored; it's the interpretations of third parties. They are opinions, not truths. I'll give you a simple example: when it has rained for twenty-one days in a row, a farmer will complain about having too much water falling from the sky when it also rains on day twenty-two. However, if it has not rained for a month, a farmer will be very happy when it starts to rain. Is rain therefore a positive or a negative experience? It depends on how you look at it! It depends on your circumstances at a certain time in a certain place.

ACCEPTANCE

You have the ability to decide intelligently what it is that you want to do. How do you do that and how do you accept the loss of your wife? Well, the secret of accepting your loss starts by knowing that you never will. So don't bother with the search. You won't find acceptance of your wife's death. Acceptance is an agreement to experience a situation or a condition without the attempt to change it, or to protest against it. Intellectually you know you cannot change the fact that you're spouse has died. However, in your heart you will never agree to it. You will always revolt at the idea. Although it is not possible, you always wish you could change it as long as you live. That wish blocks you from accepting your wife's death, and that is perfectly fine! However, you can find another acceptance. If you're willing to, you can accept the fact that you can live your life without her. How painful this may sound, your life is not over yet. If you choose, you can create a new future. A future, which doesn't include your wife physically, but it surely holds her spirit.

VALUES

If you're ready to do this, begin with clarifying your personal values. Only when you are clear about your values, are you able to take effective decisions. Focus on what's essential to you in your life. Do you want to be happy, connected, generous or adventurous? Or is it important that you are passionate, elegant and dynamic? If you're not clear about what's most important in your life, you will not be able to rebuild your new life. It starts with your values. So how do you determine your values? Again, start thinking about who, how and where you really want to be. Learn how to perceive your thoughts and emotions as they are, not what they appear to be or what you think they should be. Then transform your thoughts into values. Only by living and doing what you believe is right will you be able to support embed a value. Hold on to these principles. Live by them every single day of your life. Don't let external influences like people or circumstances have a grip on you. Instead, always focus on your values. Once they are anchored, they will function as your deepest levels of drive and motivation. The question you have to ask yourself regarding formulating your values is therefore, "How does this value help me in making my decisions?"

Don't betray yourself by not following your values. You can test them, but don't ignore them on purpose. You'll only be fooling yourself. These principles are who you are. By being aware of them in every situation, you always will be true to yourself.

In my search for comprehension and willingness to simply go on with my life, there were three values that served me personally the most.

Value 1: Optimism

The first value is optimism, meaning to be able to see the possibility of a positive outcome in any given situation. I'm an optimist. With whatever I do, I always trust the end to be positive. This attitude has helped me to be hopeful for getting out of this horrific episode in my life. Of course I doubted if I could continue to be optimistic. How profound can a value be? Well of course it is profound, otherwise it wouldn't be a value. It implies by definition a deep, powerful and personal commitment. You identify yourself with real principles. They become part of you as you live your life through your values. In traumatic situations like losing your wife, when nothing is as it seems anymore, you try to hold on to your inner core; the real you. You search for something familiar as all reason has disappeared. No wonder you stick to the values you have distinguished. They don't just disappear. Later on I understood that changing your values is a matter of choice, but I liked to be optimistic. I recognized myself as such, and so I hung on to this principle. It was important to me. Besides, I always loved life. I did not believe life by its very nature was miserable. There were parts of life filled with tragedy obviously, but I could not accept that life, as a whole would be about suffering. In addition, I believe in the power of creation by human beings. I know that there are more people creating and structuring their lives and their futures, than there are people heading for destruction. Most people take small steps to try to improve their lives. Even if it's a struggle, somehow they find a way to advance. Homeowners rebuild their properties after they have been destroyed by hurricanes and flooding, and on smaller scale mothers help their kids with their homework. All these, are accomplishments with the hope for a better tomorrow. We don't exactly know what that day is going to look like, but somehow we trust it can be a better one. This mindset allowed me to be persuasive in my attempts to find a new way to create my new future. I share this with you because I think it's crucial to your long-term success for whatever direction you decide to go.

Value 2: Passion

Passion for me is one of the most beautiful expressions of emotion. It is so fascinating to see people acting out of passion, whether it is professionally or privately. It is the state of intensity and the devotion in which people do or create something that I find extraordinary. Passionate people don't worry whether their actions are right or wrong. They don't even think in these terms. They are emotionally so attached to their cause that they are determined to achieve the outcome they have projected. Of course they won't always produce a positive result, but that doesn't seem to bother them and it appears that it is totally clear what they want to do and how they have to do it. I have noticed that every time I conducted something with passion, the gratification afterwards was so much more fulfilling. Passion is a powerful value. You are actually not just doing it for the result. You act because you love the action. This for me is the best way to live and persevere through difficult situations, which allows me to do what I love to do. Passion is also very inspirational. Other people love to be engaged with someone who is passionate. Passion feeds the hope of people, and passion is timeless; as long as you are passionate for something, you aren't limited by time. You lose yourself in it.

Value 3: Compassion

The third value I want to share with you is compassion. *Com*passion has the depth and magnitude of passion, but compassion isn't directed internally. It's directed toward someone else. Unlike passion, a word that's focused on thoughts and on desires, compassion is all about action. Compassion is what you bestow on others; it is an expression of caring and concern. It is developed inside of you, and it doesn't have any effect until you apply it to others. It's no good being compassionate if you never do anything for anyone. At the same time, I would like to stress that in order to demonstrate effective compassion for others it is first of all necessary to be able to experience and fully appreciate your own suffering and to have, as a consequence, compassion for yourself. The Buddha is reported to have said, "It is possible to travel the whole world in search of one who is more worthy of compassion than oneself. No such person can be found." When I arrived at my parents' place the day I was informed about Judith's death, my dearest friends were there immediately, although it was during a working day. They just dropped everything they were doing in order to be at my side. I will never forget that. By being compassionate, these people have taught me what it means to care and to give. The feeling they gave me of not being alone after all, led to my wanting to be part of the world again. I understood I wasn't just by myself. It has inspired me to try and do the same for others.

If you live your life by checking the fact if your thoughts and activities live up to your values, you'll be true to yourself. Determine therefore carefully the values you want to live by. If you have more than one, search for balance between them. Don't focus on just one of them. Instead spread out your attention. Moreover, do not search for confirmation whether or not you've picked a good value. Your values come from within so they are always the right ones for you. What is important to you doesn't have to be significant to someone else. That doesn't make it good or bad. As we differ from each other physically, mentally and spiritually, our values will also be different. So make sure you don't just search for people or circumstances that meet your values, but live them. If gratitude for instance is a principle, make sure that you are grateful. Think well about values and don't hurry. Take your time and follow your heart. You will feel it when the right value arrives.

§ 2.3 MOVE ON

It took me quite a while before I understood that it is up to me to determine what story I put in my mind and how highly important is what I think. In addition, I found out how much the concept of time holds us in its grip and how our values determine our state of mind which link back to our thoughts. Knowing all this, I was finally able to focus on how I was going to re-create my life. I was aware of the fact that I wanted to make a difference and to share my story and know-how. I wanted to leave a legacy. I sat down and thought carefully about the moments where I had been most productive in my life and I imagined the times when I was really inspired by my activities. What came naturally to me were images of people who I helped developing themselves personally, and from whom I received some amazing feedback in return. At the same time, I thought of all the times I met, saw and heard people talking about the loss of a dear one. It occurred to me that women talked more easily about this subject. Men kept it more to themselves, although I knew how they felt. I understood that the volcano inside was damaging them. It was keeping them from creating a new life emotionally, spiritually, mentally and therefore physically. I wanted to help them to unblock themselves. I understood the importance of adding value to people's lives.

We saw that in order to change anything you have to be aware of your situation and you have to understand the rules, which mark your playing field. If you're not happy with where you are and you want to exchange it for another place, it is paramount to know what causes your unhappiness. Once you know that, it's nothing more than calculating the steps toward your desired direction and figuring out how to take them.

However, although you might think the only reason for your discontent and uncertainty of your position in the world right now is the death of your wife, I challenge you to think a little more. Sink a bit deeper into your thoughts. The death of your spouse is the knock out punch you've received, but there are surely some more hits, which have preceded this KO. Very often the demise of a loved one is the tip of the iceberg. It is your job to find out what's beneath the surface in order to have a clear picture. I know this is not easy, as your conditioned mind has made up stories, which justify any hardship or nasty experience. However, be honest to yourself and be brave in confronting some ghosts. Once you've succeeded in doing that, you just have to do one more thing: you have to take action and move onto your new path! However, people are creatures of habit, which simplifies things. In the years together with your wife you've created a certain routine, a habit of doing things, even a schedule. You have identified yourself with that life, as if you and your wife were hooked into one and the same life. With the death of your spouse you have also lost the life you've identified yourself with. This is another reason why you feel disconnected. Even the small simple ways of how you had organized your life are not there anymore. You feel like hurricane Katrina has visited you and she has completely destroyed the life you knew. You now have to come up with a new way of getting things done. You have to find new anchors that will fasten you into the soil of your new world. These anchors are the foundation on which you build a new strategy and a structure for a day-by-day increase in the quality of your life. They will be the basis of your new personal identification.

UP OR DOWN?

As we've discussed before, when people confront personal tragedy, they normally show one of two states. They can give up or they keep on going. If they surrender, they decide that the hardship they have suffered is too much to bear. They are totally overwhelmed by emotion and are blind to any possible solution or way out. They close themselves up and eventually they burn out like a candle. In a way they play it safe. To play it safe can be a healthy strategy. It is what most people do. Unconsciously, we let other people take most of our decisions so we don't have to take responsibility. If we have no other alternative, we just buy insurance to cover ourselves. Most of us, in fact, live the lives other people have projected on us. This starts with our upbringing. Our parents tell us what to do, choose our school and teach us what is right and wrong in the world. Together with the people in your environment such as friends, family and neighbors they then project a future image of your life, which you should follow. So you do as you're told. After finishing high school you start working or you go to a university. You find a girl, buy a house and work long office hours. You follow what the media are telling you and every couple of years you can vote for some politician who, again, promises to take care of you.

As a good boy, you believe what other people say to you as long as you have your important things in life: a house, a car and a couple of days vacation with your family.

Others, on the contrary, rise above their usual self. They use the experience and the emotions as leverage to find the energy to display that maybe they have lost the battle, but they surely did not lose the war. They take on a more adventurous style.

Once there was a boy with a huge sense of curiosity. Like the other kids of his town he went to school, and learned how to read and write and as they were living at the sea, the kids were taught how to draw charts. These charts would show sailors the blueprint of the coastlines in order to avoid hitting any rocks. In addition, it showed the way to sail to other countries. Now this boy wasn't your everyday kid. He was adventurous. At a very young age he already wanted to sail out, but only as a teenager did he finally have his first sailing experience. The captain of the ship loved to talk about far away destinations, and so the boy was full of excitement. At the same time he was studying the great names of ancient times. The boy read scripts of philosophers like Pythagoras and Aristotle who claimed the earth was round instead of flat as common knowledge dictated. The boy thought about this idea over the years and when he became a captain himself he actually shared his thoughts that the earth was spherical. A round earth would supply the opportunity to sail westward instead of going east in order to reach India. People laughed at him, but Columbus didn't laugh. For almost twenty years he stood by his conviction until in 1492 he proved he was right.

Taking a stand isn't always easy. It can make you feel quite lonely. In order to follow your dream you have to show determination and you have to be courageous, yet the pay off is so much sweeter, knowing that you have done what you had planned for yourself and that it was your dream that brought you here. Doesn't it make sense to live *your* life? Honestly, how could you live someone else's life? How would you do that? When we think about the quarrels in our lives it is almost always because someone is not living up to the other person's expectations. How exhausting it is to always meet the requirements of other people. When you have to answer to someone else's demands all the time, you constantly use your energy in favor of that other person. We all know the feeling of "this totally wears me out". Certainly it does. It is a forced way of living; it's not smooth at all! On the other hand, when you do something that you love, in which you put all your passion, you are full of energy at the end of the day! You just want to keep on going! The conclusion would therefore be simple: put on your Sunday clothes and go out there to find some adventure! Start to live your life by doing the things you love and share your energy and passion with others. Now, this is a nice theory. In reality things aren't that boosting currently. I get that you wonder why on earth you should find a way to continue at this moment. I understand that you feel completely lost and alone. You don't even know where to begin.

Let me guide you here, and take advantage of the fact that I have already been down this road. Don't waste precious time on being angry at life or on self-pity and indifference. You have already noticed that life continues no matter what. Your life goes on anyway, but don't go driving with the handbrake on. Take it off and go on smoothly. Let me worry about being your navigator for a while. You have just to decide where you want to go and I will show you how to get there.

By sticking with me so far I suspect you are or you want to be part of the second group: the adventurers. That's perfect! Let's go!

UNRAVELING THE WIDOWERS' MANUAL ANCHORS

In order to start a new life, you have to develop a new version of "you". To do this, I offer you tools, which I call the "Widowers' Manual Anchors". You can use these anchors to securely attach yourself to solid ground in order to keep from drifting off so you can focus on firmly building your new you and your new world. Once you are solidly grounded, you have to shine a light on the road you choose to follow so you can clearly develop your actions and activities. Without a clearly lighted path, you will stumble and fall, your anchors will loosen their grip and you will finally drift off as a ship does in the night. Therefore, just taking notice of these anchors won't do the trick. You have to take action and apply them. The anchors are five ways in which you can fortify your mental state in order to take on this immense confrontation you're facing. My first aim is to get you firmly back in the saddle, but it's not just about getting up. To get up is one thing, to start moving again is another. It's not only about examining how you've got on your back, that's pretty obvious. It's how to look up, understand the opponent and to figure out a way to conquer him. Knowing that this opponent is probably one of the biggest adversaries you will ever meet, if not *the* biggest, don't you agree that to take on each and every new challenge from hereon would be definitely doable, perhaps even easy? So, let's take a look at the anchors. These five pillars describe how-to-do, how-to-be and how-to-become a stronger version of yourself. I will show you how you can influence, change and control your own life. With your permission, I will do so in order to help you turn your life around in a way that gives you reason, knowledge and energy to face this new path in front of you.

Anchor 1 Feel: I will address the importance of experiencing the pain of the loss. Even though you just want to run away from it, the pain can serve you. I will show you how this works and how the pain can help you in getting ahead.

Anchor 2 Share: it's important to tell people what has happened. Do not hide yourself from the world; rather be part of it. If you don't share your story with other people, you will find it very difficult to move along.

Anchor 3 Dare: in order to exit your current condition, you need the help of other people. Don't think you're strong enough to handle this on your own. It takes courage to ask for aid, and to tell the world you don't know how to handle your situation.

Anchor 4 Meet: create a special environment for special people you meet and share your ups and downs with them. Pursue your road to happiness. Not everybody you meet is going to agree with what you do or don't do. Don't let that put or hold you down.

Anchor 5 Care: we will see that contributing to others is both inspiring and compelling. It is an opportunity to make a difference in people's lives. However, not only to care for others, but also why and how you should take care of yourself is critical. I will address the foundation of the outcome of our results: our self-worth. The way we think is based on how valuable we judge ourselves. This means that the higher we classify our worth, the more successful we eventually are in life.

STEPPING OUT OF YOUR COMFORT ZONE

Now I know there's a good chance that you're still not sure what's up and what's down. After you've read all this you could likely say, "Yeah, whatever, I'm not ready for this, and even if I was, I just don't feel like building right now. I feel miserable and I just don't give a damn!" Besides that, the emotional burden that comes with the death of your wife has cost you so much energy. You're totally worn out. How could you possibly start to work on creating a new future when you're on your knees? You wouldn't ask a marathon athlete at the finish to run another twenty-six miles. You are so messed up; you hardly know your last name, so to speak. Even if you wanted to, mentally you would not be up to the job of constructing a new life right now. Isn't it just much easier to follow the outlines of society? Isn't it less trouble to have others telling you what to do and where to go? At least you don't have to think, since someone else is doing that for you. "Give a guy a break!"

No! It is not easier to follow other people and I will not give you a break. You are already broken enough! I want you to do one thing: *I want you to live your life*. Don't make compromises here. It will only make you lazy. Laziness won't get you into action and without action you will not have the results you want for yourself. Follow the anchors and you will be able to whirl less and head more directly to wherever it is you want to go.

When people die, there is no grief protocol. Sometimes, depending on religion, there is a certain way of organizing the funeral. Yet when that's over and everybody picks up where they left off a couple of days before, you find yourself standing in a strange and unknown world, alone. Now, once again you could crawl into a little corner somewhere and hope that no one will notice you. You could say, "I play it safe and I definitely avoid getting myself into painful situations", or you can take a deep breath and face this new place. Of course there's a risk. You have to step out your comfort zone. I know that's scary, however, with this attitude you are much more likely to find gratification. So which will it be, which do you think will bring you more happiness and fulfillment? After answering this rhetorical question, why don't we just get started with the first of the five anchors?

Chapter 3

FEEL

PAIN IS SOMETHING RELEVANT. It is essential in our lives. It is a protection mechanism of the body. It gives us the message that you're in a hurtful or dangerous situation: you should leave immediately! Nicely put, but where in the world is the exit in our situation here?

I've told you I went into a blur the first few days after Judith had died. I felt like I was watching myself on film. Intellectually I knew I was there, but I didn't actually feel present. I missed out on a lot of things that happened around me, and I didn't get everything people were saying to me. I do however remember the phone call from the undertaker that my wife was "ready" to be visited. A week after she died she had been flown over from the Far East. I hurried to go and see her at the funeral home. There was still a part of me that didn't believe the fact that she was dead. No, let me rephrase that: a part of me didn't *want* to know she was gone. At the same time however, I wanted to make sure that she was "okay". I wanted to see if people had been treating her with respect.

When I arrived I went straight into the room where she was. I saw her lying in her coffin. She looked strange. Her face, which was normally an explosion of expressions, now was emotionless. "What are you doing in a coffin", I heard myself thinking. "Get out of that box! This is ridiculous. You're twenty-six years old. We've got things to do!" I took a chair, sat next to her and I took her hand. There were no tears, just silence. My head understood that she was gone. My heart did not. I was speechless, even in my mind. Her body was present, but her spirit had left; yet it hadn't gone far. I remember that I felt a strong presence in some way. I couldn't place it very well. I was not sure if it were my head spinning or if I noticed an actual proximity of an intense energy. In any event, I didn't pay attention to it for very long. I just looked at Judith in a white dress lying in a coffin. I don't recall for how long I sat there, but when I looked up, I saw some of my friends who were standing around me. They had joined me at the wake. I saw them crying and I wondered why I wasn't. I know now that I was still in shock. The blow had been so hard that my nerves were still paralyzed.

NUMB

Though the ability to experience pain is essential for protection from injury and recognition of the presence of injury, at first I didn't feel it. It's a phenomenon known as "Episodic Analgesia". This may occur under special circumstances, usually in the action of sport or war: a soldier in a combat zone could feel no pain for many hours from a gruesome amputation or other severe injury. They don't always have the possibility of getting immediate treatment and somehow have to find the strength to move to safety in order to survive. The brain is actually capable of blocking out pain; the person is intellectually aware of the injury but doesn't feel it. You will recognize the sensation of pain but suffer little, or not at all. In my case, I guess my brain decided that the death of my wife caused so much pain that it was just too much to bear and shut off all doors to the nervous system. Once the immediate danger has passed, the pain will start to intensify, and boy it did! It became a psychogenic pain. This is pain caused by mental, emotional, or behavioral factors. It can actually cause physical pain like headaches, back pain, and stomach pain. Sufferers are not always being taken seriously, because the general public tends to think that pain from a psychological source is not "real". It is therefore important that you learn to share your story. By telling what has happened, others will understand your physical and mental state better. I will get back to that later on. However, specialists consider that it is no less actual or hurtful than pain from any other source. People with long-term pain frequently display psychological disturbance. Self-esteem, often low in chronic pain patients, shows improvement once the pain has been resolved.

Does this mean that if you were to live the rest of your life in pain you would never overcome the death of your wife? Does this mean your self-confidence is permanently damaged? No, would be the answer to both questions. The pain will remain, yet it will decrease. You know it's there. You will understand it won't disappear. Yet you can learn how to function and grow while being in pain. So how do we handle the pain?

1) Accept the pain for what it is

We have talked about the secret of acceptance. We know that accepting the death of your wife is practically out of the question. As long as you hang on to the wish of altering the circumstances, which would bring her back, you won't fully accept the fact that she's gone, which is perfectly fine. However, my goal for you is to have clarity and empowerment. I don't want you to have a clouded vision because you're too busy avoiding the pain. That is why it is crucial to understand that your wife's death can be a source of pain for the rest of your life. If you will accept that and if you step away from the urge to change the fact that you are in pain, you will free your mind to focus on constructive things. It will most likely not go away. It will become less dominant, much less even. Yet every time someone mentions your deceased wife or asks you if it still hurts, you probably will confirm it does. You have to if you're honest, and it will be so also after fifteen years.

So try and accept that the pain is there and don't try to run away from it. It will take too much energy and in the end you'll find yourself in the same situation. So accept the pain as a given fact and free your mind to focus on productive ways to sort out your life.

You accept something by simply not questioning it. Do you wonder whether the sun will rise tomorrow? Assuming you have no trouble walking, do you ask yourself if you can get up from the chair you're sitting in and answer the doorbell? These are proven facts to you; you don't even think about them anymore. If you would be afraid whether the sun rises and whether or not you could lift yourself from that chair, you would be extremely preoccupied. You'd probably lack the energy and the time to engage in other activities. Instead, you don't worry about these "basic" facts of life, because you simply have accepted these certainties. No doubt it's a subconscious choice, but it's a choice nonetheless. It's the same with accepting the presence of pain. If you want to be able to center on being in a constructive state, just choose that it's all right to be in pain. Now, it doesn't take a lot of training in order to come to this state. It is a decision you take.

Imagine yourself going on vacation with your buddies. You are about to go to a golf clinic in Barbados. You have packed your bags and your clubs, and now you are awaiting the arrival of your friends in order to go to the airport. You're full of energy and excitement. You are in a very positive, dynamic and vital state. How did you do that, easily, you chose to be. What you are about to do is fantastic according to your rules of having a good time. So you smile and you feel the adrenaline pumping in your body. Unfortunately, upon your arrival at the airport, your boss calls you. There is a problem at work. You are the only person who can solve this problem, and if you don't see to it right away, the company is going to lose a major deal. You have to go back now! Immediately your state changes. Your energy level sinks below zero, and with a heavy heart you feel like bowing your head. You are really upset for having to break off your vacation.

What happened here? Five minutes ago you were high upon a cloud and now you are all the way down? A different picture is what happened. Going to Barbados with your mates was changed to heading toward the office to deal with some problem at work. When you enter your office, your boss awaits you with a big smile. So you get even more upset as you assume your boss is even enjoying the fact that you had to cancel your trip. However, as it turns out, the problem was just solved by someone else. First you would be angry with your boss for not coming up with this solution earlier, but then you'll realize that the coast is clear and you are allowed to continue your vacation after all. "Barbados here I come!" And from one moment to the next, your dynamic state has returned.

This example shows that being in a certain state, whether it is resourceful or destructive, is merely a choice. You know pretty well how to be in either one of them. Therefore when you are confronted with the theory, "Accept being in pain", it is also just a matter of choice. It only requires flexibility on your part, and being open for other options. There is not just one truth. In fact, in my view *the* truth doesn't exist. There is just opinion. So opt for this one: Open up your mind for other possibilities and think through if your "truths" are still real. One of them would be to avoid pain at any cost. If you decide to turn from that one, you're on your way. Accepting that the pain will be always a part of your life is a big decision. We have been taught to avoid pain. It is part of our knowledge, intuition and reflexes. So when I ask you to go against that, you resist. That's a normal human reaction. You are at least curious about the "why", but you will probably feel a stronger desire to learn more about the "how to" ignore this rule.

LOOKING GOOD

Normally, when people take big decisions, they take a lot of time to consider and reconsider. They want to find out how much this new decision contradicts their standard rules. Well, you know, it doesn't. A rule, as we've seen, can be altered in a split second. Just let go of it, or come up with a better one. However, there is another difficulty hiding around the corner: If you would be able to change your rule so easily and dismiss this problem, how much of a predicament was it in the first place? You might say, if I don't find it that hard to live with the pain of the loss of my wife, it could send a message into the world that I'm not in that much pain. Wow, stop, this is your mind talking! It wants you to look good for other people. Remember, it has nothing to do with your decision to accept the pain. You do so because you understand it will remain in your life until your final day, and you know that it would take a lot of energy trying to get away from it. In any case, ultimately you would not be able to solve the problem; the pain would still be there, and in the process you would have wasted all of your energy. Don't worry if you look good. Eventually it all comes down to the way in which we communicate with ourselves and what actions we produce. Be honest to yourself, and authentic. That's what inspires people, and that is what looks good in the end.

2) Don't let the pain get you off track

Focusing on the pain taught me an expensive lesson; I had mixed up the pain with money. This is what happened. Not too long ago I attended a seminar lead by T. Harv Eker where he shared an interesting view with regard to the way we think about money. In fact we have a certain blueprint in our minds that controls the way we manage our money. One of the ways that influenced the construction of our money blueprint is a specific incident: did a particular event occur that had a strong impact on how you relate to money? Well, I guess so! In my case I had received money from Judith's life insurance on the house we had bought together, and unconsciously my mind had linked the pain of losing my spouse with receiving the insurance money. So as I was trying to get rid of my pain, I mistakenly got rid of the money. Now the money is gone, but the pain is still there! Of course it is. To be in pain has nothing to do with having money or real estate or other things. It is not possible that you can exchange one for the other. It is no use that in your desperation, you try to buy your way out. It doesn't work that way. I understand that you don't care for money right now, but that's temporary. It surely keeps its value in our society. There's going to be a day that you want to be a full member again, so don't throw it away. If you want to make a difference in people's lives, money will sustain your projects and your message. If you can't focus on what you want to do and where you want to go, refrain from managing your money. In fact, my advice would be in case you receive some insurance money, put it away, don't touch it for quite some time or trust someone else with it in order to invest it in a safe way. Practically, if you have to organize any administrative issues like insurance, housing etcetera, ask a friend to help you. These things show up most of the time not long after the funeral and you could definitely use a clear brain to sort things out.

3) Use the pain as leverage

To deal with pain because of loss is new to you, and you only can start coping with it when you have actually become a widower. You may have read about it, or watched documentaries regarding the subject. Yet, eventually you must learn by doing. Although it has not been your choice, this is the time to start learning, and as with everything we start doing, our first attempts usually fail. Don't beat yourself up for it; allow yourself time to progress by making changes in your trial and error approach. Go out there, try and figure out a way that you think might work for you. When you're done, you evaluate the result. Everything that doesn't work, you leave behind in your next attempt. To learn how to deal with pain to this extent is like learning everything else you were taught in life. First of all you have to recognize the challenge for what it is: what are you up against. In this case it's easy to identify: pain and being scared to deal with pain. It's not just being in pain today, but even more the fear to be also in pain tomorrow, which blocks you from getting ahead. You are afraid the pain will last and simultaneously you hope it will pass. This worrying is merely your old mind trying to hold you back again. They are nothing more than conditioned thoughts formed by experiences of other people stashed in your head with only one goal: to keep you right where you are.

Anyway, don't blame your mind for being afraid. There is always freedom of choice! We will never reach our full potential until we stop blaming, or praising for that matter, other people for the outcome of our actions. You are responsible. Our pain is not caused by the fact that we have set our limits or expectations too high. We are in pain because our rules don't meet our reality check.

What you need to do now is to use your pain as a turning point.

You need to open your eyes and look for alternative routes and then use the pain in order to inspire and motivate yourself to actually take the first step into a new direction. You have been living up till now with what you knew so far. The death of your wife brings out a new ball game. In order to play well, you have to let go of your old you and invent a new one. If you manage to get to this level, you will be ready for whatever challenge you face in the future.

IMAGINE

How do you do that? Well, by imagining your new you in your new world. Start by picturing yourself already there. Have a clear image of how that looks and feels and watch the details. Details are very important. List the details on a piece of paper. When you have done that, you can make a plan of how to obtain each one of these details. For instance, you have pictured yourself in a certain environment or habitat. What did this place look like? Were there any buildings? Was there water? Did you see other people? What did they look like and what were they doing? By getting the answers to these questions, your new place will be more tangible to you. It is then a matter of looking in the real world for a place just like that.

The next steps for you to take are to come up with a tactical activity plan on how to install yourself in this new place. Nothing fancy, just list what you need in order to go and to be there, and then get to it. When you search well, you will find it.

In chapter eight I will outline a roadmap, which helps you in getting you on your way.

4) Embrace the pain

We know why people are always trying to avoid pain. It's a natural, human instinct. We are afraid of pain. Now, besides learning how to cope with it, I would suggest that you take one step further and embrace it; embrace the pain. Change it to a sensation of pleasure. Feel it, be happy you are in pain. To feel pain means that you are alive. Look at it in the eye and then just step toward it as if you would let it rip you apart! The more you love your wife, the more pain you feel. So I grant that you suffer enormously. Smile at your pain, and laugh at your pain. The hardship you have experienced is beyond normal human pain. Nothing in the world can ever hurt you again. Once you realize this, you'll notice that pain itself is irrelevant as to living the life you want. The sensation of pain itself has no actual meaning.

Remember that things and activities only have meaning if you decide to give them meaning.

You will notice that you are not scared of being in pain anymore. You understand that fear is nothing more than worrying about a possibility of being in pain in the future. However, if pain itself is irrelevant to you, so is fear.

You overcome fear not by trying to run away from pain, but by mastering it. So get to know your pain thoroughly and give it a new meaning, a resourceful meaning. Pain can be the foundation of your new future when you transform it into the love you felt and feel for your wife. In this way, an extremely powerful foundation will be the base for tomorrow's world that you will build for yourself. The love you have for your spouse is indestructible; not even death can tear that apart, and so will be your groundwork. You can do this easily by linking the idea of pain to the love for your wife. An enormous sense of pleasure now displays itself in your mind. As long as the intensity of the image is present, your mind doesn't know the difference between reality and fiction. You will actually feel good! If you get to this point, you'll feel practically indestructible. You will have so much power and you'll be full of energy. Now the idea is to shape this energy into positive developments. Think of how to create a new project for a new future and then you just act on it.

Start doing it, don't wait until you think you have put all the pieces into place. You never will so begin now! Be open-minded, positive, and energetic and believe that you can do it. To believe that you are up to this starts with thinking that you can. You still wonder if you could do that? Well, I did it and I'm just a normal guy. So if I can do it, you can too! I don't want to make this any more difficult than it has to be. Think that you can shape a new and great future for yourself. This thought will convert into a belief if it's strong enough. A belief itself is very powerful. If you believe you can design a new future, you will put yourself in a state that is going to actually bring you the results. In this way you will be able to develop a roadmap that will guide you toward your goal, but not until we have dealt with a few other mindsets. We'll get into that in the next chapters.

However, first I would like to introduce to you the WMA and the WMB. In the WMA, short for Widowers' Manual Anchors, I will give you a short recap of the elements we have discussed in the previous chapter. With the WMB, the Widowers' Manual Beacons, my purpose is for you to give it a moment's thought, reflect and take action. Take a break from the world and create a time and place just for yourself. Then go through these guideposts in order to start lighting the way toward a clear and resourceful state in which you can start to build your new life.

WMA FEEL

1. Accept the pain is there

2. Don't let the pain get you off track

3. Use the pain as leverage

4. Embrace the pain

WMB FEEL

1. I am willing to accept the pain for what it is because ...

2. The image of my new world looks like ...

3. The new image of myself looks like ...

4. I am not afraid of pain because ...

Chapter 4

SHARE

INITIALLY, THE WAY JUDITH had died was highly problematic for me. I found the circumstance of her departure humiliating and totally disrespectful. She was stabbed to death, and normal people don't get stabbed. This you see in films or you read about in newspapers: criminals killing each other over drug money or something illicit. Yet this was the most beautiful and loving girl you could imagine. She was always full of joy and energy, touching people's hearts with her enthusiasm and her caring. And she was murdered? I couldn't deal with this thought. I wanted to hide myself as far away as possible from anybody. I didn't want to talk about it with anyone. Addressing the details of her death would drive me crazy. It not only collided immensely with one of my top values, respect, but I was also afraid people might think badly of her, as if she would be one of those criminals. That assumption alone already made me furious, so in order to protect her and myself from outside opinions I sought solitude.

Amazing how much a self-created story in your mind can mess you up! It is really destructive, and it doesn't matter how you've lost your wife, whether it is after a fatal illness, a car accident or in my case a homicide. A catastrophic story that you invent in order to survive this ordeal can take you out of the game for quite some time. Even in case of much less dramatic storytelling, it is very common to search for solitude after you've lost your spouse. After all, who really understands what you're going through? Who relates with the fact that you're one big emotional mess. Moreover, guys don't easily talk about their emotions, at least, not with other guys. However, we do appreciate friendship. Being friends sometimes is as strong as marriage, and they are there for life. True friends won't let you down, not ever!

1) Don't hide yourself

When we talk about the importance of sharing your story this would be a first category: don't hide yourself. Socialize and be present! Be part of the world. Go and visit your friends and talk to them about how you feel. Share with them that you are scared or hopeful. Whatever the subject is, do not keep it to yourself. I encourage you to especially share those issues which you find the most painful to discuss. Not talking about the fact that she was killed, has cost me so much time. Besides the fact that I was totally in denial about her death, I was stuck in my conviction that the world might think that Judith had somehow brought this upon herself, because decent people don't die in that way. Therefore I kept on repeating the same reason to keep things in the dark: not talking about that and how she died would be the best thing to do. The problem, though, was that there were two forces pushing against each other.

On the one hand I wanted to share my story. I needed to tell people what had happened just to get some of the load off of me. I also knew no one has gotten better from keeping secrets. In effect it kept me from developing my relationships with others. I felt I did not give myself totally as I did not share my whole story. The death of my wife was of course present in my every day's thoughts and performances. It was a life-changing event, which influenced the way I looked at the world and how I acted and behaved in this new place. My anger and frustration resulted in misbehaving, being cranky and at times being very impolite. So, by informing people that my wife had died I could have received some understanding. I don't want to excuse myself for my behavior as this also is a choice, but it is sometimes easier for others to know where you're coming from in order to help you. You wouldn't want to put a band-aid on someone's knee when they are suffering from a migraine.

On the other hand, I was convinced that not sharing this story would help me to keep myself sane.

Now, what do you get if you put two opposing forces up against each other? Nothing, you won't move! You will stay stuck where you are. Imagine two equally big Sumo wrestlers trying to push each other away. They stay exactly in the middle of the "Dohyo", the circular ring that marks the playing field of the wrestlers. Only when one of the two redirects the force of the other, movement appears.

Therefore, in order to escape the situation where you feel stuck in the middle, I would advice you to create some movement by sharing your story. The reason for not sharing would be avoiding pain, as bringing up the subject would confirm that your wife is gone. Denial would change in affirmation, but whom are we kidding? We chose to move on with our lives, so let's move on. Go out there and start talking to your friends. Don't be skeptical to "use" them, as being friends is a strong emotional bond. So if you want to talk about how much of a mess you are to your mates, just do that, and be confident in them. As a matter of fact, they will appreciate your openness. At the same time, inform them that you don't expect any answers! It will put them at ease. Besides, they have not been taught how to deal with these matters. Yet here they are, ready to support you for a long period of time, so share your story, your feelings, your dreams or your lack of conviction, and give them the benefit of the doubt. You will live through this phase in your lives together and you will all come out stronger. You'll be even better best friends and you'll learn how to tell your story. I'll give you an example.

ECLIPSE CHASERS

Thirteen years ago, two colleagues and I decided to go to one of the places in Europe where you were able to see the 1999 solar eclipse best: the North of France. We left Holland in the pouring rain; it's funny how bad weather bonds. The goal was to escape the clouds and to chase the solar eclipse. We drove for a couple of hours and just before the last piece of the moon was sliding over the sun, we parked our motorbikes, fell on our backs in the long grass and simultaneously stopped breathing at the exact moment the moon blocked the sun. It was almost a spiritual moment: there we stopped being colleagues and began being friends.

After that we went on numerous different motorbike trips throughout Europe and it became clear that we connected easily with other people through our passion for motorcycles. When you show passion for one thing, you create an opening to talk about another. It is in circumstances like this where you can tell your story and what it has caused in your world.

The more you share your story, the more feedback you get, the larger your spectrum becomes, the better you become in telling your story, the more you will share your story, etcetera. I'm talking about sharing your story with your friends, real physical friends, and not online social network friends. Make sure that you really meet them. True human interaction is the key. How many of them stopped what they were doing and rushed over to you the minute they learned what had happened? How many will still be at your disposal a long time after you have lost your wife? The ones who do that, those people are your real friends. Besides, spending your days behind a screen watching the lives of your mates in 2D won't improve your life substantially. It can only contribute to your self-development to a certain extent. Yet in order to reach a certain outcome we have set out to get, we have to take action. We can prepare and develop ourselves for a lot of things online, but eventually we have to engage our activities in the real world, the 3D world. For the record, I have nothing against social network sites like Facebook and Twitter. In fact I understand the importance and the usefulness of social networks in our society, and it's a great way of sharing your story, but usually I prefer a hug over a tweet.

2) Stop assuming

Losing your wife is one thing, losing your child is another. I lost my wife that day; my mother-in-law lost her daughter. Now, I don't want to compare one to the other. There's no point in making comparisons between two horrible perspectives. However, I have had the chance to get re-married. My mother-in-law did not have the chance to get another daughter. I don't mean this disrespectfully; it's only an objective observation. Somehow I have fixed my life again: I found a new wife and I became the father of a beautiful little girl. I have filled the big dark hole in my life. The gap in the life of Judith's mother is still huge. I didn't realize this as such, until I became a parent myself. Her pain must be immense. I cannot even begin to imagine what it must be like for her. So I feel for her and I do that by paying my respects.

Shortly after I had met my current wife, I went to Judith's mom to tell her that I had found a new girl. This was a difficult moment for me, as I almost felt guilty, as if I was betraying my first wife, her daughter. I was extremely influenced by the opinions of others regarding a certain time that I had to stay single before getting serious with someone new. The opinions of others almost choked me when they were saying things like, "You cannot bother your mother-in-law with this news! It is too soon!" However, I was convinced that I would create more harm by not telling the facts than if I would share them. So I went to her and told her the news. She took it really well, smiled at me, wished me luck and asked me if it were hard to tell her this news. She was wise enough to understand the impact the voices of the others had on me and she wanted to reassure me that everything was all right. I was really glad I had told her about my new girlfriend and I realized how important it is to communicate and how big-hearted some people are. Over the years I have always stayed in touch. From the very first year I have sent a card to my ex in-laws in the month of June. I did this until a couple of years ago. As a matter of fact, I re-married an Italian girl and like all Southern Europeans, Italians have a more religious culture. She taught me that there's a Saint for every day of the year, and so I searched and found the day of Saint Judith. I decided to send her parents a card on that day instead of the day of her death. A Saints day is a happy day, a day of celebration instead of a day of mourning, and I want to celebrate her life by living my life to the fullest. Her mom and dad really appreciate my gesture and the story. There is not one year that I skip this tradition and I know how important it is for them, and for me. Now, I know that sending a card to your in-laws can sound silly, but as long as you mean well, people will appreciate your effort. The people around you have lost their daughter, their sister, their friend or their colleague and for them it is essential that she has been important to you. You can show that with simple gestures. Be natural and authentic in your approach. Keep them informed about the developments in your life. If you have difficulty in informing them about a certain development, just tell them that. Also they have already lived through their worst day. So grant them a little credit, they are surely up to it.

Stop assuming! Whatever it is, it is like fortune telling. It is a waste of energy. People never say or act the way you assumed they would. Instead whenever you want to share your feelings or just some information, ask questions. Open yourself up. Your bravery will be acknowledged and appreciated. It is really important for people to share their thoughts and feelings. It gives them the idea of making a difference. You can realize this simply by listening and acknowledging their stories. These could be anecdotes from people who had a business relation with your spouse, or chronicles from old school mates for example. Exchanging tales can create synergy, which will help you in many other ways in the future. The secret here is to stay in touch. Stories will come up as time passes. If you keep the contact, you will learn about these experiences. The impact your wife has made on the world, therefore, remains not only in the past, but lives into the future. Who knows what parable will cross your path? In the meantime, stop thinking and taking decisions for others. That's not only foolish, it's also arrogant. I have never met a mind reader and I don't think you are one? You don't know what goes on in someone else's mind, as they don't know what goes on in yours. Therefore, when people meet you for the first time, they don't know that you're a widower.

REALITY CHECK

I had kept my wedding ring for quite some time after the death of Judith and I remember a painful incident in a restaurant. I had a bite with a buddy of mine and we met another man that he knew. They started talking about family and things. Suddenly this guy noticed my wedding ring and he asked me, "Ah, you're married too I see! How are things in married life for you?" Obviously he didn't know what had happened. My friend was embarrassed and as I wasn't really following their conversation, I was taken off guard by his question. "Um, well, okay I guess", I heard myself stumbling. This was quite another reality check for me, and it hurt. Of course I didn't blame the man, but I quickly left the conversation anyway. Thinking back, I should have informed him that I had lost my wife, and that it was all right for him not to know how to respond and that he was not to feel bad for his question. Yet I've learned from this and I had the opportunity to act more adequately a short while after that.

THE APPLICATION

About thirteen years ago I was applying for a job as a Customer Service Manager with a big publishing company. I had my job interview with the Commercial Director and a HR officer. They wanted to know, as a future manager, how empathic I was. So they gave me an example of a staff member who had lost her child. I answered that being a widower myself I was very positive I would be able to show my empathy without any trouble. The two were frozen on their chairs, no doubt because of the fact I gave the news quite bluntly, but also, because they did not expect this; I was only thirty-one years old; not an age where you would expect someone to have already lost his spouse. I then explained what had happened in a more descriptive way, which relaxed them somewhat, although not totally. Anyway, I got the job, partly as I was honest and brave enough to share my story with them, partly because I was simply the right person for the job. I positioned myself with authority and I convinced both people about the strength and the added value of empathic leaders.

The word empathy is derived from the Greek word "empatheia", which means physical affection, passion and partiality. It is the capacity to think and place yourself into the inner life of another human being. Empathy is about impulsively and naturally tuning into the other person's thoughts and feelings. You can distinguish two major elements to empathy. The first is the cognitive element: it shows the ability to understand the other person's feelings and the capacity to conceive their view. The second element to empathy is the affective element. This is a spectator's relevant emotional response to the other person's emotional state. We perceive others as empathic when we feel that they have accurately acted on our values, and our skills. We find other people empathic especially as they appear to acknowledge the significance of our actions. In professional organizations people work together with primarily the same challenges, hopes and fears. These human elements don't stay out in the parking lot while their owners enter the building to start the working day. Decisions at work are highly influenced by an individual's perception. Companies have to be aware of that. They have to know how to deal with the human aspect of their workers. In order to develop a sense of teamwork, companies need therefore to change their focus and search for empathic leaders and co-workers.

CLAIM YOUR ROLE

However, change is something that most people raise their eyebrows over. When you want to change a situation, you will immediately find yourself with a lot of obstacles in your way. Obstacles placed by others who are quite comfortable where they are, or other people who don't exactly know how to organize these new ways. Therefore we need people who stand up and share their voice on this. We need people who give us clarity and direction, not only on a professional level, but also on a human level: people who understand the importance of both head and heart; people who passionately bring credibility from a certain experience; experts who have known personal hardships; and people who have actually experienced the power of emotions. So if you decide to stand up and combine your professional knowledge with your empathy, you will identify yourself as a new leader in your field. Don't play it small; it doesn't serve anybody. Do not think you have to lower yourself in order for others to feel comfortable. Despite the current circumstances, stand up straight and be a beacon for yourself and others. Inspire people with your story and emotional drive. This is the time to do so; this is your cue. Go out there and claim your new role in society.

3) Position yourself powerfully

Don't play the victim; people want to be inspired. Usually inspiration comes from passionate, energetic people. The ones that complain about everything and anything are not seen as exciting and thrilling. So when the subject is on the table, talk openly about it. Don't put up a show, be authentic and real, but also be dynamic and strong.

To position yourself strongly is a very important element in your development. In the introduction of this book I already stated that people don't like to talk about death. It is almost a taboo. The media love to show death and misery on TV because lots of people probably like to see how others suffer. Yet when it comes too close, they back off. Therefore, when you announce that you've lost your wife, people may want to run away. If the person you're talking to actually thinks that the subject is taboo, it means that he or she adopted the rule that it is somehow not permitted to talk about death, and because you are willing to discuss it, you do something improper. For many people that is frightening and therefore they want to leave the "crime scene" as fast as they can. So how would you handle someone's taboos? Well, you don't, you can only handle your own taboos because it is not something physical or tangible. It's not clearly specified; it's more a feeling you have about the fact that some things you just don't do or certain subjects you just don't discuss. Because it is culturally adopted by a large group of people it is very difficult to question it. It is really hard to convince someone about the fact that you actually *could* talk about this matter. Factual arguments won't stand their ground in this case. It is your job to explain them that it is all right to talk about death. You do that by giving your audience a role model. You have to show them, again in an authentic way, that in spite of being in pain you are full of life.

When you display that you're not a sad and lonely person whom they'd better avoid like the plague, you can put your audience at ease. If you share your experiences and feelings in a powerful way with a strong voice, forceful body language and through the use of positive words, your listener will first be surprised, then intrigued and eventually inspired.

STORYTELLING

An audience will better perceive your story when you tell it vividly. Now, the question is how can you put yourself in a state where you are genuinely vivid. You would need some leverage in order to put yourself in a challenging position. You can do that by following three simple steps Bo Eason taught me.

First, you must love your story so much that every time you tell it, your emotions will automatically color it. Don't fake this; people will know and feel when you're not authentic and you will lose them. Love the heartache and love the idea that you will rise like a phoenix from the flames. Because you will.

Second, make your story as personal as you can so the listener will easily identify him or herself with it. That shouldn't be a problem in your case. Open yourself up and stick your neck out; people love the brave hero who shows his vulnerability and who is willing to face fear.

Third, go back in time to when you first experienced your story and pretend as if now would be the first time you tell someone about it. Give yourself with everything you've got and do not hold back.

Do not allow yourself to lose one ounce of excitement because you have already told this story a couple of times before.

These steps require a certain physical back up. It is impossible to vividly convey your story and be a stoic reporter at the same time. People will not believe you; they don't even want to believe you. If you want to touch your audience's heart, stand up! Don't sit down, as you will lose fifty percent of your credibility. Get up, move around the room, use your space and be present! Support your words with your body language and use the different tonalities of your voice. Bend over when you speak softly and widen your eyes. Stand up straight when you firmly announce you have survived this bitter quest and give your crowd the feeling as if they have too. Take the people with you in your story and make it their story.

Be a storyteller that people remember; be a storyteller that they love.

If you would shine your light with brightness and warmth over this subject, you will create a strong base for developing your new future. It will, however, take time. In any event, those who will be touched by your story will continue the conversation. The ones that aren't, were just passing by.

4) Choose your words well

Be careful how you communicate the fact that you've lost your wife. People do not expect that kind of news. Remember that they will interpret your story differently from how you see it. You have lived the experience, they haven't. Be natural, pure and careful in the choice of your words. What has happened is paramount. The death of your spouse leaves an impact! This event changes you forever. Notice that I use the word "change". You're not worse off; you've encountered a new experience. Be aware that when you share your story not just the subject leaves an impact, but also the words you use, words are powerful. Think carefully how you are going to tell your story. Focus on certain terminology, and be attentive of who's in front of you, who is listening to your story? Carefully tell people your story and teach them about the impact it has had on you. Share your story with care and do it fully. Do not hold this information back as it will hold back your development and your growth as a person. Maybe they won't say it out loud, but people are grateful for your words. By sharing your story you will support them, and your support will teach them how they could deal with emotional subjects. So teach them about your experience, and how they can deal with you. Educate them as to how they can enjoy their lives, and teach them how they can appreciate their lives. Be a world-class teacher. You can do this just by telling your story. It's not important to give advice to someone, as people will make up their own minds anyway after hearing you talk. Just share openly what has happened and what the impact has been on you and the people close to you. You will receive amazing feedback, which will help you to move forward. Tell people it is all right for them not to know what to say. Trust me, there are really only a few people who know what to say in these circumstances, but tell your story anyway. Share it with the world. Write about it on your blog. To share the pain reduces it by half. Besides, you will not be in a good mood all the time. There will be moments - birthdays, Christmas, restaurant encounters, etcetera - in which you will be confronted with the empty space in your life. This will have an impact, forever. So it is important for people to know what has happened. At least they will understand why you're a bit awkward that specific day.

At times your tragedy will frighten people. However, every so often people will surprise you with true compassion and sometimes you even find yourself in situations where your story works out to your advantage. Realize that people are ready to listen to you. They are interested in hearing you speak about this subject. Death is one of the most frightening things in life for people, because it's unknown and we are scared and skeptical of things we don't know. So if they have the opportunity to find out a little bit more about your emotions, they will be a little more prepared themselves when they lose someone close to them. At the same time they can empower you with their responses, which you can use the next time you share your story with someone else. In this way you create synergy; being a teacher gives you the opportunity to be a student as well. Share your story, learn simultaneously, and always remember that the way you say your words, is the way your life turns out.

WMA SHARE

1. Don't hide yourself
2. Stop assuming
3. Position yourself strongly
4. Choose your words well

WMB SHARE

1. To share my story, I would have to …
2. The way to reveal myself in my environment is …
3. My plan to position myself powerfully is by …
4. I will physically use my body to share my story like this: …

Chapter 5

DARE

ONCE I WAS SITTING DOWN with a Life Coach. I told him what had happened and that I found it difficult to talk about the event. In fact I was completely closed up. Initially I had told him that my wife had died, but not how. I had constructed a thick iron wall around me to keep everybody out, but it was also keeping me inside! I was illustrating the words of Jim Rohn, "The walls we build around us to keep out the sadness also keep out the joy." The coach asked me if we could do an exercise. He told me to close my eyes and to imagine a beautiful place on earth.

The coach asked me, *"What do you see?"*

I answered, "A beach."

"And what is on the beach?

There is a beach club. I'm the owner.

What's going on at the beach club?

There's a bunch of people sitting around, having drinks and enjoying themselves.

All right, now there's one guy sitting at a table, and he's not having fun at all. What do you do?

I go over to him and ask him if I can help him.

Why?

Well, being the owner I feel it is my business and responsibility to make sure everybody has a good time in my beach club.

No, you cannot help him. What do you do now?

I'll ask him again if there's absolutely nothing I could do for him.

No, there's nothing you can do. What do you do now?

I'll leave him alone."

The coach told me to open my eyes. He smiled at me in silence for a couple of seconds and then he asked, "This guy at the table, it is you, isn't it?" In a split second I understood the meaning of the exercise. The coach said, "I guess you just don't want anybody to help you. You think you can deal with this on your own. Maybe you're right, but in my opinion, this is a little bit over your head. Give people some credit. Even if they didn't lose somebody, they still can be of help to you in a lot of different ways. Put yourself open to them. What do you have to lose, and stop being so damn arrogant." I still feel the emotion of that moment. Plus, he was right about my being arrogant. I was deciding if others could manage the news or not, which was definitely a wrong move. I would advise you not to be so cocky that you determine what's good or bad for the other person to hear. You would only do this because you're afraid that no one will listen to you. Feelings like arrogance are nothing more than a lack of self-confidence. Anyway, it's normal that you close up after what you've been through. You have been hurt so much; you don't want to feel like that anymore. You cannot feel like that ever again, so you protect yourself by shutting yourself off from the world. However, this protection keeps you from interacting with other people, who could otherwise help you take the next steps.

1) Show your vulnerability

The example above shows you again how your mind can fool you. If you hide so no one can see you, no one can help you either. Now, to put your head in the sand like an ostrich is naïve, but to be aggressive like a dog locked up in a cage is not the answer either. Lower your guns, the fight is over. Focus on how you can be productive and have the courage to ask for help. Dare to show your vulnerability and people will actually help you. Look out for help and you will find it; remember: what you focus on expands! People are very curious to know about your experience. As I mentioned before, death is something people find interesting. You can tell them firsthand how it has affected you, so lay off your macho image. You thought you were a tough guy in your old world, and that being a man means that you are able to handle any problem. However, in your new world being tough means telling others how, where and when you hurt and being brave enough to ask for help. You could start by asking questions as to whether or not you could inform your audience. Do they have questions about the event, about how you feel, or how you cope? They probably have, but as long as most people treat the subject as a taboo, they will lack the courage to come up to you and ask how you are coping. So take the initiative yourself, and create a safety zone for a conversation in which you both feel comfortable. This way, you put your audience at ease and consequently you will have a more meaningful dialogue. You will motivate the other person to think about his or her own position and activities in life. As you will again receive a lot of feedback, this will lead to improvement in your life.

2) Learn to receive

Why is it so difficult to ask for help? Well, perhaps when you ask for help, you usually get it. Maybe therein lies the problem? Maybe the challenge is not just asking for help, but also to receive it. If you are a poor receiver, you don't ask for anything. The difficulty in receiving help from others could originate on three levels: competence, control and reciprocity.

One of the main reasons why people find it difficult to receive is because they think they don't deserve it. This would mean they have a problem with their self-esteem. People might be afraid that by asking for help others might see them as weak, needy or incompetent. Of course we live in a highly competitive world. Our society teaches us that if you let your guard down, you'll get hurt. In addition, to display that you don't know how to do something could be used against you. Yet, we need to put things in perspective here. It's one thing to ask for help in a competitive business environment, it's another when you ask for some level of assistance when you've lost your wife. Stalling won't help you here; it could make things even worse if you wait too long to seek help. The ostrich strategy doesn't work very well. As long as you don't want to think about it, you won't know how to handle it, and it is in the how-to area where you will find the answer. Normally, what most people do, is to link security with competence. We are comfortable in the things we know and in the activities we know how to perform. So if we have to do something out of our comfort zone, we back off. The reason for this is because we know the outcome of our standard familiar activities and we don't know what is going to happen when we start on something new. Yet you find yourself on a totally different playground here. The way it was doesn't exist anymore. If you want to have some positive results for your new life, you have no choice but to play this new game. You can do this with a great deal of competence, because it's new and therefore you're the one who decides the outlines of the game. You are the one who sets the rules. You don't have to live up to someone else's directive. No one is going to judge you when you ask for help in these circumstances. The chances of failing and being punished are non-existent here. So go ahead, ask away.

Usually men have a harder time asking for help than women. Guys need to be ambitious and tough; society demands that of you and so do you. You think that you don't need anything or anybody, and it is beliefs like this that withhold us from asking for help. Yet, not only do we want to be seen as the tough guy, it is also important to gain control of every situation. Probably we think that when we ask for help, we will in effect be surrendering some level of control.

The person who is assisting you could take over and to give away that power is frightening to most of us. However, this has everything to do with having enough courage to show how vulnerable you are. Yes you are down on the ground like a professional boxer in the ring. Besides being a rule of the game it is a gentlemen's agreement that you don't give the guy on the floor another kick in the head. If you communicate clearly what has happened and how you are in need of aid, people won't do anything but help you. There is no issue whatsoever regarding who's in control. So don't strain your brain over this one.

Nobody likes to be in debt. Asking for someone's help could shift a power balance in the relationship. Some people think it would be unbalanced if you ask for help as you obviously have nothing to offer in return. Nothing is farther from the truth in this case. You have lost your spouse; do I really have to remind you about your current position? Do we really have to talk about balance here? There is no such thing as balance right now, that's why you're so messed up. You are totally off balance! However, this is your starting point. The person in front of you who is offering his or her help has a different reference. After giving you assistance, he or she could ask for something in return. Yet I don't think this is the time to worry about that. It's about your recovery. It's the flight attendant telling you to put your oxygen mask on first. When you will be able to return the favor, you will, but that's not today. So just say, "Thank you very much, I appreciate your help."

3) Have the courage to let go

The first ten days or so after Judith died I spent at my parents' house. After that I wanted to go home. Home, now it was just our house.

Together we made it "home", and that was not the case anymore. I remember coming through the door in our empty house. We bought it only six months earlier. At the time it had seemed to be our dream palace. It was a small, little white cottage with a thatched roof, a garden with a pear tree, lots of roses and a boxwood hedge. Now it was nothing more than four walls and a roof. I recall that moment as one of the times I felt totally alone on the planet. I was sitting in the living room at the fireplace staring outside the window. I thought, "Alright, I'm ready, you can come now." I was waiting in silence, a deafening silence. I waited and waited, until I realized that I had to let her go, but I couldn't.

Yet, what did I hold on to? Besides memories, personal items and a lot of pictures, there was nothing. Well, there was something, something significant. Something that ripped my heart out over and over again: her scent. Not just her perfume, but also the scent of her body. It was lovely and devastating at the same time. I wanted to bury my head in her pillow and simultaneously run away as fast as I could. I sat on the couch watching the roses outside and was thinking, "How do I solve this? How do I walk out of this place and take her with me?" I became aware that leaving the house would be in fact taking the first step in letting her go. I racked my brain thinking what to bring with me, but then I understood, that it would not solve anything. In effect, trying to grab hold of the past keeps you from moving toward the future. Try to walk forward while looking back over your shoulder. Sooner or later you hit a wall, literally. Of course I didn't realize this on the spot. It had been ten days since I became a widower and only three since I had buried my wife. It was impossible to let her go, I just couldn't. It has taken me years to put her personal items away together with her pictures. Not all of them, but most of them. However, every time it was saying goodbye a little. Each time it is hurtful. Honestly, I don't know whether you should box everything all at once not too long after the funeral, or as I did, step by step. In any case, it is about letting go; letting go of the past that is. You don't let go of the love for your wife, but her life stopped and yours continues. Letting go shows that you understand that. If you don't let go, it means that your life stopped as well on the day she died, and that's not the case. You keep on going, you just do, so do it!

In any event, you're the director of your own life. You choose the moment, when and where. It's okay, it's up to you, but choose, and if you choose, choose for life, your life.

I do understand where you are right now. You are afraid that when you go on where she left off, you might lose her forever. Therefore you search for a way, which avoids that. You try to hold on to her by holding on to her personal items, to her photos and to the objects you purchased together. Yet these items are not your wife, and they don't determine whether you feel well or not. You are the one who decides that. It's a false hope when you cling on to these objects and think you will be all right because of their existence. It's a story you've made up after your wife died. It's a way of protecting yourself from the pain. However, all these items are nothing but items. Of course they represent memories, but these memories live inside your head, not in these particular objects. You would only need them to trigger your recollection, but memories are by definition all in the past. It is obvious that clinging on to the past won't serve you either today or tomorrow. Cherish your one-time images, yet in order to create a new path I advise you to let go. It will give you peace. Letting go will clear your mind in order to be able to energetically create the availability for new developments. Think of it as a stick in a relay race, the stick being your life. It is now being handed from the previous runner to the next, from your old world to the new world. The race is not over until the finish line and you're not even half way, so keep on running and make the previous runner proud of your accomplishments. You could organize a small ceremony if you wish. You can do that alone or invite some other people. Pick a special place and those items, which were dearest to your wife. Place them in a setting that pleases you together with a lighted candle. Put on your wife's favorite song. When the song has finished, you think of her, give her an air-kiss and you blow out the candle. Then you say out loud as a declaration, "It is okay like this. I'm letting you go. Take care, I love you."

However, when you have just lost your spouse, you are mainly functioning on automatic pilot. You are partly unconscious in your thoughts and actions. The danger exist therefore that in order to keep you in your comfort zone, your conditioned mind will constantly tell you things like, "What is the use of this all?" or, "I will never get out of this mess." The answers you will produce, will keep you just where you are right now, so wake up for your own sake! Ask yourself questions like, "If I don't change what I'm doing now, what will be the result?" and, "How will my life be if I will develop that activity even when it seems extremely difficult at this moment?"

Again, don't assume, but ask questions. If you don't know how to do something, figure it out or ask for help. Also in case you do know but you're just not able to handle a specific situation or activity, ask for help. It will save you time and time is valuable as we saw. Remember that the quality of an answer depends on the quality of your question. When you ask a positive question, you'll get a positive answer. The opposite is also true. Be aware of what you ask. "Why did this happen to me", will not trigger a positive answer. "How can I use this experience", opens up a constructive internal dialogue, which will lead more likely to an effective outcome. Have the courage to create new and empowering questions. I dare you to do so.

WMA DARE

1. Show your vulnerability

2. Learn to receive

3. Have the courage to let go

WMB DARE

1. I will show my vulnerability through …

2. I am a good receiver because …

3. I am competent because …

4. My communication is positive because …

5. I will organize a "let-go ceremony" on …

Chapter 6

MEET

AS TIME PASSES BY, your urge to live will increase. Perhaps and hopefully after reading this, you will really understand that today *is* the first day of the rest your life, and it's just too bad not to live one day fully. You are going to notice more and more that it is important to you to share your life again with other people, perhaps even with one person in particular again.

Yes, I know, you are not interested in a new relationship. That's it, book closed. You might even feel offended just by the fact that I bring this up. It's how I felt the first couple of years. Even after her death I was still emotionally attached to Judith only. But stranger things have happened. You could meet this new woman! Now, if you do, don't wait too long before you also tell her what has happened. It might scare her off, but your story is too important not to share with her. It is part of who you are now. Show people that you deal with this matter in an intelligent, emotional and dynamic way, and not just in the case of a personal relationship. Also business partners

81

with whom you work or are going to work on a daily basis could and would benefit from knowing what's happened. So how are you going to bring the news?

1) Create a special environment for special people

In case of a possible new girlfriend, understand that your story is your own; it is how you see it. It is your interpretation of the facts. These interpretations are fed by your past experiences and the ones other people have "lent" you. Your friend has a totally different perspective. She will therefore interpret your story differently. Her reaction will be different than you expect. You will not encounter a right or wrong reaction. They don't exist. Everybody is doing his or her best at the time to give you a proper reaction. People can say intelligent things, they can have emotional reactions and there are some who don't say anything at all. This last one will be the most frequent reaction you're going to receive. Like I said before, most people don't know how to react when you tell them you're a widower. They don't expect that. So in your new lady friend's case, it is imperative that you recognize her effort in giving you a reaction. Be supportive here, and put her at ease. Make sure she feels free to ask you whatever question she has. Again, it is a difficult subject, as we have never learned how to deal with death. So don't expect to have a trained Life Coach in front of you. It is crucial for her to be as relaxed as possible about the subject. Only then will the two of you have the opportunity to grow into this new relationship. So put her at ease, make her feel special, and really show effort. Why is this critical? Well, if you truly want to pursue a long lasting relationship with her, you have to convince her of the fact that you want her for herself. There cannot be a doubt in her mind about that. If she has one, try to eliminate that or break off the relationship. This may sound blunt, but if she is not assured that you are interested in her specifically, she might think that she is nothing but a stand-in. Then her insecurity about being the "number two" will always remain a problem between the two of you. You will keep on having false discussions about comparisons between her and your previous wife. You will find yourself squeezed in the middle of something surreal. I will come to comparisons a little later on. Anyway, let's say she's with you one hundred percent. Sooner or later you want to introduce her to your family and friends. Remember that I spoke about you being everybody's widower? Now she's going to be everybody's new girlfriend. So I urge you to help her with her introduction to your family and friends. There can be strange opinions about how you should behave as a widower as we've covered previously.

PUBLIC OPINION

In general, people have difficulty in accepting change. Your environment has been seeing you for years with your wife. Even after she has died, the two of you are still together in their minds. The moment they start to get used to the fact that you are in fact alone, you suddenly show up with someone else! This means that they have to adapt their own image of their role in your life again and that can cause difficulty. Be aware that people can react quite strangely, even radically. Your environment can be truly happy for you for finding this new girl, but at the same time there might be people who could be offended by it. Maybe even the very same people! They could have created a role for themselves in your life after you've lost your spouse, in which they took care of you and for which they have been receiving your attention in return. Now your attention will go to your new girlfriend and that will require a new adaptation for some people. Remember that also they have experienced a great loss. This death concerns your wife, but to others she was a daughter, a sister, a dear friend or a colleague, and because of the fact that they have been preoccupied with your recovery, they could have been neglecting their own sorrow. This will be revealed to them as soon as you "release" them from duty because now, *in their perception*, you have someone else to do their job. In their newly gained spare time they could find themselves facing their own pain all of a sudden. In addition, perhaps they fear your wife's memory will disappear because you have decided to continue your life with someone new.

In any case, I want you to be aware of the fact that they could take this out on your new girl. Of course it has nothing to do with your girlfriend. It's all about them and their mindsets. Therefore make them understand that your feelings toward your wife will never change, that she will remain in a special place in your heart. Share with the people of your past that you understand that they also hurt, but that you hope and trust they will allow you to have a new future. Yet there can still and probably will be tense situations. Again, know that it has nothing to do with you or your new girlfriend. It has everything to do with the rules of your family and friends raining down upon you. One of the best things would be, to introduce your new girl individually to them. In a small context people behave and communicate with a more open mind. They are more willing to show their real selves. It's more intimate and genuine. You accordingly create a better atmosphere and the fundamentals for a healthy relationship. Your family will also feel more important as you've decided to inform them individually and personally. So be the host of the meeting of two worlds. Make sure the people feel appreciated and listened to. Just remember that when you take care of your new world, it will also take care of you.

2) Share your ups and downs

If you've found and let a new girlfriend into your life, realize that she is not just a part of your new world; together with you she is the architect of it! Don't pretend you're all right all the time. You cannot ignore your pain and sorrow for the loss of your spouse. Don't try to hide that from your new girl. We've talked about the importance of feeling the pain. Don't forget those guideposts when you meet a nice girl. If you try to deny your pain, you will live a false life. Be open about your feelings. Ask if you can talk about them. If she allows you to do so, your new relationship will be strong. If not, I'm sorry, but the chance of success in the long run is going to be quite small. You see, your deceased wife is always going to be part of you. Know that you do have more room in your heart to love another woman. Be sure you communicate that to your new girl, as she will be insecure from time to time. Especially because she will for instance notice the pictures and other physical memories you will have of your wife. It could make her feel uncomfortable. Discuss that, and explain to her that your house is not a museum of the past in which there is no room for the future. In fact, why don't you put some new pictures of the two of you next to your old ones? In the end, they're just pictures. It's whatever story you make up which make them easy or difficult to look at. Whatever you do, acknowledge her and make clear to her that there are two worlds for you: the old one and the new one. She has not been part of the old world, but you are very happy to share your experiences from it. Clarify that it's not a competition between the two worlds:

which is the better one? Better does not exist, there's just different and difference makes our lives interesting. It gives color. Make sure she understands that. Reassure your new girl that you love her for who she is. Explain that both your new girl and your wife are charismatic women and that each one has and has had her unique and wonderful qualities. Yet to compare the two would be like comparing a Ferrari to a Maserati; which one is the better or more beautiful car? I don't know, you tell me! However, it's quite normal for your new girl to ask herself if she is in the same league as your previous wife. Explain to her it is not a very resourceful state she puts herself into. It will only feed her insecurity. Therefore stay away from comparisons. It's a lost cause; you will feel like Don Quixote fighting the windmills.

Involve your new girl in special occasions like your wife's birthday or your wedding anniversary. These days will be painful for you, at least during the first years. Time heals the wound, though the scar remains visible. So as the years pass, you will deal with the loss of your wife differently, also on the special dates. Tell your new girl directly what you have in mind to do on those days. Do you want to go to the cemetery? Do you want to spend some time alone, or do you wish she would join you? It's not a one-way street. Allow your new girl to express her feelings too. Allow her not to agree with you. You don't have carte blanche just because you're a widower. If you want a relationship to succeed, the two partners have to be equally positioned. Plan vacations to exotic or adventurous places that neither of you has ever visited. Combine your holiday traditions, and create new customs that will become unique to your new relationship. Redecorate your house or even one room at a time together, or buy a new home and make it your own. Take the lead in proposing to accommodate the memory of your past together with your new girl so you can both grow from it and from that your new relationship.

SOCIAL ANIMALS

As we have discussed previously, everybody follows the rules they themselves have adopted or created in their lives. Past experiences, study and upbringing have formed a set of standards people live by. However, it's not one hundred percent fixed, and neither is yours. So don't get upset that someone close to you could react to the fact that you've found a new girlfriend in a way you would not have expected. Especially in a post death situation, which of course is very emotional, people's reactions can be stronger. Take a look at your rules and decide whether or not you can re-define them. Once again, communication brings the solution. Go and take this person in a one on one setting and discuss matters. Do this with everybody who disagrees with new developments in your life, no matter how ridiculous you might think the issue is. You'll notice it will be a discussion about rules. It is going to be a discussion on how you are supposed to do things. Explain that in spite of the respect you have for this person's personal opinion, his rules aren't yours. They never can be. At the same time inform him that he should also respect your views on life and as such your activities. Explain that it is your life that you're trying to rebuild. The old world is not there anymore. The only way to pursue your life is by taking the road ahead of you. It is no disrespect toward your wife or to him, but it would be disrespectful toward you and your life if you wouldn't go ahead with it. People are like plants; either they grow or die. There's nothing in the middle. So, you continue to move forward or you perish in the end. The place that you've visited just after your wife died was so dark, that you decided not to stay there anymore. Your decision is to create a legacy of which you will be proud, of which your wife would be proud, and you hope that others will support you in doing so. Either way, it's up to you to build your new life.

A new relationship is natural in my view. It simply matters because we are social animals; we live in groups. So if you wonder whether or not you should go out there again to partner with someone; I would say without a doubt in my mind, "Go for it!" Don't be frightened to take action. Action is the bridge between your inner world and the outer world. Maybe you are afraid of loving and losing again, but remember that fear is just an anticipation of pain. The occurrence has not happened! It's just your imagination, it is "Mr. Mind" again, trying to do its job: protecting you. Yet the secret of freedom is not to believe your own mind. It is not necessary to get rid of the fear, because it won't go away. Instead, act in spite of fear. When you face fear, look at it and move straight toward it. Just do it! Go and live. Maybe you will get hurt, and if you do, you just go on again! That's how you live your life. Don't think too much; your real intellect is in your heart, not in your mind.

WMA MEET

1. Create a special environment for special people
2. Share your ups and downs

WMB MEET

1. The special people in my life right now are …
2. If I want to design a special environment in order to submit my story, I would …
3. I engage my new girlfriend in developing …

Chapter 7

CARE

I WAS DRIVING IN my car about nine months after Judith had passed away. There was a lot of traffic. Suddenly I had to break as I saw a line of cars appearing in front of me. Oh no, please not now: a traffic jam, and I was already late for my appointment. I got really upset about it. I was even angry at the other drivers for taking this same road at this hour. Looking around for a way out I saw someone smiling in one of the cars. I remember asking myself the question what this woman was smiling about, and then it hit me. Not another car, a breakthrough: I was mad. I was angry at something as usual as a traffic jam, something that occurs every day! It's full of traffic jams, all the time! So why did I get myself all upset? Yet I was, but then I started to smile. I slowly understood that I had a breakthrough. If I could be angry at something so ordinary, so common, as a line of cars standing still on the highway, it would mean I was on my way back to the "real" world. After nine months of disregarding life, I started to show some form of caring. I cared for the fact that I could be late for my appointment. That meant I cared for the person I had to see. Or at least I cared for what the outcome of our meeting could be and what that would mean to my life and to me.

In order to be respected by others, a good way to start is to simply enjoy and respect the people in your world. When I say "your world" I mean each and everyone who is present to you. That can be your family and friends. They show up in your world pretty often. Yet, it is not the frequency that is important here. Also the people who you encounter briefly are part of your world. You should also consider the girl at the cash register, or the guy standing next to you at the traffic light. In fact, everything and everybody you see, feel or hear, partakes in your world. Care for it and it will take care of you. So what are the important ideas to consider here?

1) Don't play God

When you have lost your spouse much too soon, you can peculiarly feel somewhat special. You can become a bit arrogant. You think you can allow yourself to be that way because of what has happened to you, as if you can get away with any kind of behavior. You also might think that other people are not allowed to complain about having a headache or a cold, or being in the wrong check out line at the supermarket. You can get irritated when people nag about the fact they didn't receive the promised bonus at work or when they find themselves day in, day out in a traffic jam and they complain about that. Compared to what you have been through this is all trivial! It's almost as if they're offending you. Well, let me enlighten you there. First of all, nothing happened to you; it was your wife who died. Secondly, who are you to decide what is right and wrong? Who are you to say what people can be happy about and what should make them sad? Just get off your high horse and join the rest of us down here. Arrogant people are not very popular. Arrogant widowers are even less loved. People are already avoiding you because nobody knows what to say to you, but now you even give them a reason to stay out of your way: you're an arrogant buffoon. Continue like this and you find yourself like Ebenezer Scrooge, all alone with your ghosts. Arrogance will not help you on your way out of your current situation; arrogance is nothing more than overbearing pride. It's proudly pretending you're better than the rest, knowing that you don't have the results to back you up. What's the risk here? If you think that others are not in your league, you will simply not play with them. Is the value they give to projects, hobbies, work or life in general of a lower standard according to your ratings? Is that the reason you will not join them in their activities, or could it be that you got so afraid that you put up this arrogant charade in order to protect yourself? Are you scared of death or are you scared to live?

Fear arises because we do not know how to do or handle a certain fact or activity. I cannot inform you more about death. I don't know a way to learn more about it and I'm afraid I wouldn't know what it is like after you die. Yet to live is another thing. You can learn how to do things in life. You can educate yourself in how to develop certain activities or how to create the lifestyle you prefer. Please be aware that if you exclude yourself completely from society it will harm your own development greatly. We need other people in order to grow, and we need to communicate and to work together. We need others to keep human kind alive. We simply need others to reproduce! Therefore taking yourself off the field does not work in the long run. You have to get out of the stands and play if you want to make a difference. Take action, have results and then it's time to be proud. Others will acknowledge you then and this helps you to enroll in the game even more.

Time is precious, so when I got highly irritated because I had ended up in this traffic jam, I realized I was descending from Mount Olympus to join the mortals on planet Earth once again. I understood that the conception of time was getting back its value in my life and this perception had been worthless to me for quite a while. I recognized I started to live in the real world again. There was proof and therefore hope.

2) Truly respect other people

Thinking about my own position in my world full of habits, opinions and rules made me realize why I was so shocked about the way Judith died. It was an extremely violent act. To take someone's life like that is completely without any dignity. There had been absolutely no respect for my wife, and respect was one of my highest virtues. I really valued respect, and I still do. Yet only the respect I have for people, objects or events? Does someone or something only receive my respect when he, she or it meets my requirements? The first nine months after Judith's death I would have given you an affirmative answer. After I got stuck in the traffic jam I got a clearer picture.

Let's respect each other, period. Let's respect who we are, what we think and the road we choose to take in order to grow into a better person. We can of course differ in opinion regarding what we do, but let's appreciate the diversity amongst people. Let's respect each other's reality. My reality is completely different from yours.

Does it make it better? I don't think so, but if you think it is, I will respect that.

There is of course a difference between respect and agreement. You can respect someone but totally disagree with that person's views or actions. Sometimes the disagreement is so immense that respect disappears. If someone says or does something, that is totally contrary to everything you stand for, the consideration and the appreciation for this person dissolves completely. However, this person somehow has a role in your life. He is part of your world in a direct or indirect way. Therefore if you cannot bring yourself to respect the actions of this particular person, you could always forgive him for what he did or said.

PUTTING MYSELF TO THE TEST

I had an internal struggle regarding my value of having respect in relation to the murderer of my spouse. As I said, respect for people was in my top five values, but I couldn't apply this toward this man. I thought really hard of a way to do this. I listened to inspiring people with even more inspiring speeches like Martin Luther King's "I have a dream". I wondered how this man could be so strongly committed to his cause and promoting peace if you would look at what some people did to Black Americans in the US.

However, once in a while you just have to stop looking in front of you for the answer. Sometimes it's enough to take a hold and look sideways for an outcome. In this case I thought of being responsible for the results in my life. I could not blame other people for my state of being. I therefore had to stop blaming the man who killed Judith. As I totally lacked any kind of respect for this man, I could only do that by forgiving him. And so I did. I forgave the man who took my wife away from me. Honestly, I have to say that it was not for his sake; it was for mine. So technically I am not sure if I use the term "forgiveness" in the right way here. Perhaps the term "release" is a better way to put it. If you are able to release yourself from disempowering thoughts like hating or blaming another human being, it won't cause you any suffering. You need release to move forward and bring the bar up to neutral. From that point on you will be able to fill your life with positivity and abundance. I knew that as long as I would hold a grudge against him, he would control my life in a way, and in order to build a new future for myself, I had to regain total control. So I let go; I left the fact back on June 4th 1997.

Sometimes the frustration and the anger still take over when I think about what he did, but then I also know how much power I give away to something and someone from the past and I let go again. Reacting strongly to these bygone images is due to the fact that the acceptance of the loss will never be one hundred percent. So don't criticize yourself for that. As it will come, the feeling will also go away. Focus on what positive outcome you want to achieve and commit yourself in doing so and make your new life about creating and caring.

Again, I do not respect the man's action, not at all! However, I respect my life too much to throw it away by being resentful and full of hate, so I accepted that for some reason it happened. Maybe one day I will find out why.

Respect will build bridges, which connect people and worlds. Get involved again in life, as involvement will ensure evolvement.

It is only when we evolve, that we ultimately create the world that responds to our personal meaning of life.

3) Serve and help others

By now you have probably received a lot of support from the people close to you, and most likely you don't actually realize the impact this has on you. That's logical as you are in a survivor mode, and you're fully concentrated on yourself. However, opening up to the idea of helping others at this very moment can be a great way of helping yourself. Help your family and friends with everyday things. They will be surprised when you offer your assistance, because everybody understands that you are quite preoccupied right now, to say the least. Yet, if you change this obvious pattern, you will create less obvious results. It can give you some air to breathe when you alter the center of attention from your despair to the misfortune of someone else. It puts things in perspective. Besides, when you genuinely serve or help another person, you will receive a lot of gratitude, especially because people feel for you now. When they realize that you help them because you think in that particular moment their need outweighs yours, they will learn a valuable lesson in being a human being. It will improve their life as well as yours. Contributing to others is both inspiring and compelling. It is an opportunity to make a difference in people's lives.

However, being humble, respectful and helpful toward others are not goals. They are not the purpose of your life. They are only the purpose of an action. A real goal is the projected outcome you have set for yourself which triggers you to move in a certain direction. Don't fool yourself; your goal is not a happy friend or a sports car.

It's the feeling these actions and objects give you, as they are merely physical projections of where you want to be. At the end it all comes down to *who* you want to be. What person do you have to become in order to live your life fully toward your dream? The answer to this question will clarify the direction you have to go. Once you know this, take the action, accomplish your objectives and grow in the process.

4) You are worth it

This is the most important one of all anchors as everything relies on the fact that you comprehend you are worth it. You are, don't doubt yourself, and do not question if you are allowed to live your life now that your wife is gone. Of course you are. This thought has been my biggest enemy over the years. I actually wondered, "Why Judith?" I have always thought she was a better person than I. In my opinion she was smarter, more entertaining and more caring. So why did she have to die?

Why not me?

Can you imagine a more destructive thought? If you have any interest in re-building a future for yourself, this does not help! Don't even think about going down that road! The only reason why she had to go was because the universe decided so. Leave it at that, since it has absolutely nothing to do with being worthy. There are war criminals living a long and comfortable life, and they surely "deserve" to leave this earth a lot sooner. Yet, who are we to decide who has to go when and where? It is not up to us to discuss these matters. It is in fact useless, and it doesn't add value to our time here. That road is really a dead end.

You have the right to live your life to the fullest. If you have any doubt about that, you'll be having a problem regarding your self-worthiness. Don't worry, we all have. Some more than others, but we all have our concerns whether or not we are good enough from time to time.

We have talked about how our thoughts lead to how we feel and eventually how we act on those feelings. Well, it starts with how we evaluate our worth. The way we think is based on how valuable we judge ourselves to be. This means that the higher we classify our worth, the more positive we think, the better we feel, the better we are able to perform and the more success we have in life. The outcome of our actions depends on the level of our self worth. Therefore in order to improve our results, we have to start working on the way we value ourselves. We do that by gaining awareness. We have previously discussed this theory. We have to distinguish fact from story for instance. Check for the facts in any given situation. What are the objective and subjective elements, and make sure you have an overall scan. Understand that when you rate yourself a low self-worth, it is probably due to a remark of someone else in the past. It's an opinion somebody planted as a seed in your mind and it grew from there. You probably may even have nurtured it yourself! Through the years you have been looking out for people and circumstances who and which would confirm this self-image. However, the origin of this perception doesn't belong to you. Try to find out what seed was planted and when. Gain perspective, and ask others for their experience. Have the guts to discuss this subject openly. I know this is a tough one, because you have to fully surrender yourself to the comments of others. In fact, that was the problem in the first place: you interpreted someone else's remark as the truth, but don't fall for the fact-story trap. Yes you have made up a negative story after a previous remark, but that does not mean that you have to keep doing so.

You know you could produce whatever story you'd like and you can change it whenever you want. So go ahead and ask your friends what they think of it. Ask for their interpretation. You might view yourself as being silly for having walked around with a false projection of yourself for years. The fear of this possibility could even prevent you from discussing the matter, but I think it would be even more silly to continue thinking for the rest of your life that you are what you are, based on someone else's individual observation. It was a comment based on the experience of another person created in a specific moment. Both that person and the circumstances in which he or she produced that remark have undoubtedly changed, and you still cling on to that opinion. That's not even silly, it's a waste! So don't waste even more of your time and share this issue with your friends. Remember you will be served with opinions. Watch both favorable and painful details they will supply, and at the end take out the seed. You do that by thinking of it like it was an old dirty and ugly coat you are wearing. You don't like it and you hate the way it makes you look. Yet, you think it's your coat and therefore you wear it. You have told yourself over and over again that if you would take it off, you might be cold and get sick. So you convinced yourself it is better to keep it on. However, when you finally realize that the coat isn't yours, what do you do? You take it off! There is no problem whatsoever. To understand it is not your coat dismisses all of the possible imaginative loyalty feelings you were supposed to have for the jacket. It discharges you from any "truth" you have made up somewhere down the line. After all, these convictions were based on false information and are therefore easy to let go of. So again, find out where your convictions come from, where do they originate?

How is your new situation different from the circumstances back in the day in which you took or adopted these perspectives? Are they still up to date? If so, analyze how they can support you on your new road. If they no longer truly exist, throw them away like an old coat that didn't belong to you in the first place. Don't be blind to the facts because you only look at an invented story. Instead focus on different options you have today in order to learn and grow. Please remember to choose to live your life consciously and not to keep on wandering in some bubble.

ACCEPT YOURSELF

The degree to which you value yourself depends highly on the level of your self-acceptance. In other words, do you accept everything about yourself, including your flaws, fears, and insecurities? Do you have secrets? If so, why are you keeping them from the world? In my view secrets hold you back from gaining ground, and I have had that experience. I frantically kept the way my wife had died to myself, and it has cost me a lot of energy to keep this in the dark. Secrets are based on nothing but assumptions. You assume others will condemn you for them. You are afraid that other people might think badly of you. In effect, you think you are less worthy for having a particular thought, opinion or outcome that you've produced and that's why you keep it hidden. You decide to leave it at that and to pick up your life anyway you can in order to move forward, but this would be like trying to conquer Mount Everest with a three hundred pound weight chained to your ankle. I would definitely advise you to lose the weight! It's hard enough to reach the top without it! How do you do that? How can you expect to make an honest run at improving yourself and your situation while constantly boycotting yourself? Show yourself straightforwardly to the world, present yourself proudly, and share whatever thoughts you have powerfully and with authenticity. Admit to those actions you've kept hidden for so long. Leave it to others to label them "stupid" or not. Let them judge your activities to their standards; it has nothing to do with you. Just set yourself free, and you will feel liberated. Don't wait for the "right" moment. The moment is now: do it today! Understand that before you can work at any change regarding your future, you must first completely accept yourself, and feel that you are worthy. Accept everything about yourself. Don't compare the way you look, where you live, whether or not you have a degree to what's out there in the world. We have been highly influenced by what is supposed to be the "perfect" picture, but this picture does not exist. It is a fake image to sell you things through and by the media. There is nothing or no one in the world that fully complies with these images. Perfection is just another opinion. So let it go. Don't rebel against yourself for not reaching perfection, as it only exists in your head.

YOU ARE UNIQUE

You are who you are; embrace your uniqueness. Only when you are at ease with yourself, without any secrets or hidden agendas, can you fully develop yourself into a strong person that is present in society by making a difference and helping others. I truly hope you understand the importance of this particular anchor. Only when you feel worthy will you be able to put into play the other anchors. Only then will you have the energy to open yourself up to the hard work it's going to require to take the steps you have to take. Only if you value yourself highly will you be able to wield the pain in a constructive manner. Only then will you be able to share your story powerfully and be ready to gather your courage to ask others for help. Only if you love yourself will you be ready for a new relationship and only when you feel worthy, will you understand the worth of other people in your environment and consequently will have the ability to care for them. It all starts with you. It is a chain reaction. Your image of your own value has a huge impact on your world. The higher you rank yourself, the richer your world will be, so I encourage you to shine as a beacon. Think about your qualities and successes. Don't be modest, you know a great deal. You can do a lot of things. You have already made a difference in other people's lives: in your wife's life for example. So I urge you to go out there. Your world needs you!

WMA CARE

1. Don't play God
2. Truly respect other people
3. Serve and help others
4. Understand that you are worth it!

WMB CARE

1. I will show others my appreciation through …
2. To prove to myself that I'm not scared to live I will …
3. The person I have to become in order to live my life fully toward my dream is …
4. I will get involved in …
5. I will contribute through …
6. I am worth it because …

Chapter 8

THE ARCHITECT
OF YOUR LIFE

THE ANCHORS HAVE TAUGHT you steps and actions you can take in order to handle the different problems and situations that you face. When do you take these steps? When do you actively meet new people, ask for help, stop hiding, feel the pain and when do you stop running away? When are you going to work on your anchor management? The answer is today, tomorrow and the day after tomorrow. In one word: always, it's an ongoing process. You are still a human being with your ups and downs. You will experience good and bad days. You can be handling yourself well through the use of these anchors for months, only to find yourself one day flat on your back because you fell for an old destructive habit. I know, because I have! It's the way of the world. For example, through the use of the Internet I have encountered people I did not see for years. At the time I was so busy *not* accepting my wife's death, that I didn't share my story. Of course people ask me after being out of contact for a while what I am doing, and so I tell them about my new business. In the introduction I share, of course, the death of my first wife, and so

I am again confronted with the pain and the search for words. I still have to position myself powerfully and I have to be brave enough to show my soft spot, as life is continuously testing me. That however keeps me focused. Being a widower is part of who I am now and I have to accept that. The moment I try to run away from it or try to ignore it, I will be in trouble. I have felt joy and I have felt pain. This has made me who I am and I'm excited about that. Lifelines aren't horizontal; they fluctuate like the movement of a snake. One day you're at the top, the next day you feel your feet slipping away. That's part of the learning curve. I have struggled with the same questions you are facing. The important thing is to be aware of your options and choices. You *choose* if you want to be up as it's your choice also to be down. When you understand this, you will be able to constructively build your new future.

So many times I have heard the discussion about "What you are supposed to do now that you're a widower." *Supposed* to do, and the succeeding sentence always was, "Unfortunately, there's no guidebook for widowers." So I asked myself, "Why not? Why isn't there a manual on how to act after you lose your spouse? Why isn't there a book that teaches how to get up again and restart playing the game called Life?" So I started writing. I thought of questions like, "When are you supposed to be publicly sad; when can you laugh; when do you start working again fully; when are you allowed to bring home a new girl; when are you allowed to be happy again?" In this regard I tried to please everybody in my process of recovery. I was so preoccupied with the feelings of others, that I forgot what was important to me. Even worse was the fact that I started to think for other people and taking decisions on their part. I thought of when it would be all right to be sad or happy in the company of others. Would it be awkward for them to see me like that? Would

I embarrass them? Could I flirt with a nice girl in the bar without offending anyone? Was I allowed to focus on making money? What would other people say about that? In the end of course I created a big messy situation where my friends hardly recognized me and I sank deeper into my misery.

The answer is in effect simple. There is a time and a place for everything and you are the one who's calling the shots about when that is. The secret is to be genuine and communicative, be honest with yourself and tell people how you feel and what you do. Also when you don't know exactly what to do, just say that. No one can tell you when it's time to start laughing or when you should be sad. That's up to you; it's about your state of mind. You can change that whenever you want. We go back again to the difference between facts and stories. There is an occurrence, which is followed by an interpretation. You draw up the content of that story, since you're the one in charge. You are the architect of your life. If you decide to be sad, you're sad. If you don't like that, just change your state. Understand that you're not sad because of an occurrence, as the occurrence has only triggered your decision to be sad. Your rules tell you how to be or how you should feel in a certain situation. Yet you have adopted those rules. You can also change them. There are cultures, which prescribe a one hundred day mourning period after someone dies. Does that mean that after one hundred days everybody is cheerful again? Why not fifty days, or five hundred? Do you see what I mean? Numbers and rules have nothing to do with emotions. They're just there to make life more practical, but in the end you determine whatever you want. Be sad, be angry or be cheerful, but don't put them in an order. These emotions will come and go for as long as you live. You will make life impossible when you create time frames on emotions. It's ridiculous to say that after one hundred days you won't be sad anymore. Will you then switch to anger or being cheerful or resourceful? Emotions are overwhelming, and they are difficult to control. Then again, I don't think they need to be controlled all the time. Sometimes it's better to just let go.

Do not feel guilty because you smile. If the people around you have difficulty in understanding why you're cheerful, ask them why they wouldn't allow you to smile. They will overwhelm you with their rules. Explain to them that those are their points of view and not yours. You respect them, you might even value them, but you will not adopt them. In the process, always communicate. Communication and education are the connections between understanding each other and therefore they offer the opportunity to build a new tomorrow together. The goal is to create a mutual imagination of your new future. Picture your role and the role of the people close to you in tomorrow's world. Share this vision, and be honest to yourself about who and where you want to be. Live up to your values and organize them in a new project.

CREATE YOUR OWN PROJECT

After you decide to get out there and build the best life imaginable after your wife's death, you will ask yourself, "What am I going to do, what is really my dream?" or, "Am I really happy with what I have been doing so far?"

In my case I was not. I went to business school and after I graduated I started in the corporate world working with some of the world's leading multinational companies. I've been doing so for about sixteen years. However, after Judith died I realized that making a difference in the world was really important to me. The idea of looking back at my life and knowing that I had actually mattered was crucial in the whole design of my new future, and a multinational conglomerate didn't appear in this new picture. Adjusting myself to the political rules of a big company wasn't very appealing to me. I felt more sympathy toward a smaller, more personal business scale, and so I thought of creating my own life with my own business. I wanted to help people who feel stuck and who are confused about their options regarding a possible new direction, but I wanted to be practical. I didn't want to offer another forum for people in despair. I thought that to create a project would be a great way to change my own grief pattern. My true passion was therefore fed by the wish of creating my future in a balanced and dynamic way. I needed to be the one taking the decisions regarding my life, and so I decided to start my own coaching company where I help people who have endured loss to regain clarity, energy and presence so that they effectively and profoundly regenerate toward a great and fulfilling life.

Thinking and talking about things can only help you to a limited extent. At the end it comes down to acting on what you say. So, in order to learn more rapidly how you put the bricks of your new life in place, it's important to create a project immediately after you have decided to take the steps onto your new path. It not only helps you to develop and evolve faster; it assists you in finding your new role in society more easily. I would dare to say you even need this emotionally, mentally and practically. It puts you in a spot where you have to communicate with your environment. It is a profound way of establishing your new self. It's not a cheap trick to keep you busy so you won't be thinking of your loss. Remember, I've been in the same position! I know you can't be fooled, but you have been beat up pretty badly. Your mind screams at you not to exit your comfort zone! It tells you to hide yourself from the big bad world, because in this way, it can easily protect you. At the same time, your mind will make up story after story in order to confirm that hiding is a smart thing to do. Hence, you stay where you are. Yet, that we saw is exactly what you don't want to do. We understand now that you need to be present in the world. You need people with whom you can interact. That is why now is the perfect moment to start your project. The death of your spouse is a turning point in your life. It's true you did not choose this moment in time, but here you are anyway. We've talked about leverage before. Use this irrevocable moment in your life to finally realize your dream. You have nothing more to lose, so get going!

How do you begin, and what do you start up? Well, you start with your real passion. What is it that you have been dreaming about for years? What is it that makes your heartbeat go faster? What is it that you can do for hours without getting bored? What is it that you would wake up for early on a Sunday morning?

Passion in effect could be a value someone lives by. It's one of mine. We saw that values are principles with which you identify yourself. It is crucial to be clear on what your values are. Once you know that, you can deduce your actions from them, which will lead you to a specific outcome. Therefore, values are the starting points of your plan. So let's start by laying out this road map, which, once filled out, leads you toward a new future: your future.

§ 8.1 ROAD MAP

This Road Map outlines how you can pursue your dream. Whether you want to share a project with others, or create a product you could sell, or set up a non-profit service or perhaps a spiritual project, the steps below will serve you in building the road toward your dream. This road map sets out the components for creation and communication. Your content will define the flavor. You can start immediately or you can plan this for another moment in your life as I stated in the beginning of this book. Anyway, it's here for when you want it.

Step 1) Trust your gut

Success begins with clarity and in order to be clear on what you want, you need to have your values straight. Your values are in effect the principles you live by. Although highly influenced by others, they feel as if they are your own. You know them and you feel comfortable with them. So make sure you have them defined clearly. I encourage you to do this while thinking in terms of being: interpret your goals or projects while you ponder who you are trying to be. Don't just ask yourself the questions what you want to do, how you should do it and why you have to do this. Also, think about *how* do you want to be, *why* you want that and *where* do you want to be. By this I don't mean just a geographical spot on Earth, but primarily in what kind of situations you see yourself and in what position within society do you express yourself freely and actively? Understand that values determine your direction. If you have old principles that you exchange for new ones, your life is going to change. Therefore, choose them carefully. Personally, I find that the best ones are those, which give me a tickling sensation in my stomach. I just feel it in my gut. If my emotions outshine the words to describe it, I know that particular value is one of importance to me.

Step 2) Envision your objective

What is it that you want to achieve? This is about determining your path: where are you going with all of this? What is it that you want to achieve in the end? Make sure you have a clear vision about your objective. With this in mind you then plan each step backwards as if you were disassembling an appliance until you have all the pieces on the table. Once that's done, you are clear on taking the correct steps in order to effectively move forward to your goal.

In the process, constantly ask yourself how your project is going to improve your life and the lives of the people you are reaching out for. What is it when you're ninety years old and you look back at your life that you want to be remembered for? Make sure you ask yourself positive, high quality questions. The more specific you are in constructing your questions, the clearer your strategy will be.

Step 3) Who do you want to reach?

We are social beings. The group is important to us. It gives us protection, company and sharing experiences enhances our knowledge and expertise. Of course people are extremely busy and therefore they only will be interested in what you have to say or offer when it enriches their lives. So make sure your message is valuable. It can be valuable when it's different from other messages: different in content, structure, availability, etc. When you think of this intelligently and thoroughly you will be able to come up with a unique idea. In short, think clearly where you want to be, choose your path and define your message.

It is necessary to understand with whom do you want to share your project. Who will be involved in making your dream live? To whom can you make a difference? Are these individuals, businesses, co-workers, clients or maybe humanitarian organizations? In other words, who is the group you're aiming your communication at? Ask questions to the people in this group like, "What does my project need to do for you?" You see, people in striving for a better life, want to get rid of a problem they have. For you it's essential to understand what causes that problem for these people. When you know that, you can construct your project more specifically and serve them better. Also think of reasons why people would not be interested in your dream: for example they don't understand how it would serve them, or they don't see the value, or they don't want it because they don't trust you. Make sure you tackle these issues. Be specific regarding which people you want to reach, where they live and how you reach them.

In my case I thought about my message. The people I wanted to reach by writing this book were obviously men who had lost their wife. I knew they were in pain, in hiding, in denial and very much preoccupied with themselves. I also knew this was blocking them from moving along, and since the world does go on, these men would stay behind. According to my rules this is not a good thing, and that's the reason I shared my story and perspective with you. I wanted to offer you a solution for when you are stuck in misery, while trying to find a way out but somehow not being able to get this done. Also I wanted to do this in the clearest way possible so it would be easy to digest and add value to your life.

Step 4) Create your project

You have a dream; perhaps it has been wandering around for years in your head. For as many reasons as you can come up with you have not pursued this dream. As of now, that's going to change. Now you understand that you won't need the permission or the "go" from someone else. There's only one person who decides the role you have in life and the outcome, which comes with that and that is you! The main idea is to create. Give practical back up to your dream, and take action. Take small steps, don't be afraid to make mistakes, and just create. Think "out of the box". Create your project and create your new world; in short, create yourself. Your role is to inspire, construct and produce a certain outcome for the people you aim to reach. Make sure their situation will definitely improve by using your ideas, services or products. Think while creating in terms of benefits for these people. Have confidence, which comes with mastery. Put yourself out in the world, believe in your ability to serve others and go from there.

Again, start with the problem your listeners want to overcome. Then talk about the possibility; what is the dream or vision you offer them. After this you show them perspective: you project yourself strongly as the sovereign in this field. You do this by sharing your story about your struggles and successes. The next thing you do is to outline your project. What is the specific added value you offer and how it will help your audience to fulfill their needs in a simple way? Be thoughtful to figure out a way, which serves your group the best.

Put yourself in their shoes. Think of how you would like to learn about a new project. What does it look like? In what way does it serve you? Do you offer it in big chunks or small ones, and in what frequency: all at once or over a certain period of time? The simpler your offer is, the better it is. I am not saying that your audience is not intelligent enough, but the simplest defined messages are usually the most powerful. Then enhance your message by always communicating energetically, passionately and with high doses of enthusiasm and fun!

Step 5) Share your message

Sharing your project with your audience would be your marketing efforts. "Yes, but I'm no marketer", you could say. But in this day and age, marketing is nothing more than teaching. Teach the people you want to reach or work with. Inform them about how your project serves them and how they will get rid of their problem once they use it. Put out valuable content and live up to your promise. People will be involved with you in order to change something in their lives. Identify that change and explain how your project will serve them. Be passionate in showing that your project or service gives them that change. Of course it has to be new in some way. So be new yourself, since people always want new things or information. Make sure people think of you as new and hot! How is your project different? The better you inform people about this, the more people you will be able to reach. How is your development relevant to what is happening in the world? How does your project solve problems so your audience knows how to use it? Share your message and be specific and clear in your description. Address the concerns your audience will have in using what you're offering, and don't neglect them. Talk about these concerns seriously, and be firm, authentic and real, giving directives, but always with feeling. Be you!

To learn how to share your passion through the development of activities, products or services, is in effect the same as learning how to deal with the five anchors. You master it by doing it. Then you find out what works for you and what doesn't. It is important to get going, and not to wait until you have "all" the elements in place. That moment will probably never arrive anyway. Just get on the road and adjust along the way.

So what could still be in your way in order to get really going? The answer is, "Your little voice." It is probably saying, "Who's going to buy my ideas? Who is going to listen to my story?" Well, if it is a good idea that would add value to my life I would be interested immediately! If your story were an inspiring one, I'd listen to you voluntarily! Put faith in yourself and get going! The only difference between you and the people who are successful in your view is that these people already took action and you did not. They are just normal people like you and me. They have their fun, their doubts and their fears. What distinguishes them from other people is that they haven't let their fears become an obstacle. They went and did what they had in mind anyway, *and they never gave up*! That's why they achieved the results; they started and they didn't quit, because it is only when you stop that you fail. Also these people stumbled and fell on their way up, but they decided to stick with what they believed was right. They had the guts to act on it, learned new best practices and ultimately succeeded. So it's actually pretty easy: think clearly of what you want to do, take action and continue developing your ideas until you realize the results that you want! That's what I wish for you;

to go and realize your dream. If you don't do that in this lifetime, then when are you going to do it?

WMB FOR PRODUCING YOUR ROAD MAP

1. My values in order to be the best that I can be, are ...

2. The things in life I love to do are ...

3. The topic I would like to share with the world is ...

4. The audience that would benefit most from my ideas is ...

5. My audience likes ...

6. The problem my audience faces is ...

7. I think I will create for my audience ...

8. The value of my communication is ...

9. The reason people will be involved with my idea is ...

10. What makes me different from others in this field is ...

Chapter 9

THE DOOR IS OPEN

IN THE PREPARATIONS TO write this book I have been thinking about what it takes to get my message heard more clearly, so that you will go forth and take action. As I have repeatedly stated, only by taking action will you change your world. Therefore in the past chapters I have in fact shared three basic elements.

The first element is methodology, emphasizing the how-to. I have pinpointed how to get a grip on the situation and how to handle certain circumstances you are and will be facing. I have presented you with the Widowers' Manual Anchors. These five directives have taught you how you can solidly put your feet back on the ground and how to cope with the biggest challenge you have had to deal with: the death of your spouse. To hold on to the anchors equals holding on to your towel. To put them into play means that you won't have to give up. On the contrary, they offer you the techniques in order to win this battle.

The second element is mindset, how do you think? Currently you are in pain and you are thinking how to get rid of it, because you know that once you do, you will be ready to pursue the good things in life. You will again, but what does it take to pull this off? How do you inspire yourself? In which state of mind are you the most resourceful? I hope you are motivated to answer questions like these drawn up with some of the results I got in these past years. Results I said; there were not only successes, as you have read about. Within this concept you can basically distinguish two kinds of human behaviors: one pursues pleasure and the other avoids pain. These are the two big motivational drives we have. When you do something you like, you want to keep on doing that for as long as you can. On the other hand, if you get hurt, or just the thought that you might get hurt, you will refrain from a specific situation.

The third element is meaning. I want you to understand the meaning of your thoughts, your feelings and your actions. Understand that what you are doing is important, and it is meaningful. Aim to rise above yourself; I want you to grow beyond what you think is possible for you now. When you ask yourself if a certain event is good or bad, I want you to understand that it totally depends on your interpretation of the facts. Nothing has in fact meaning until we decide to give it one. Although your first emotions regarding death are feelings of sadness and ending, you can decide that the content of the succeeding thoughts will be more productive. I trust I have shown you how to proficiently turn the experience of losing your wife into new ways in which you can create a prosperous and compelling future where you can claim a new role for yourself. You have meaning in the world, so step up. The time is now!

So here you are, ready to learn, to give, to develop and to take the appropriate action. Right you are, and I applaud you for it! There are still so many people around you who you can help, to whom you make a difference in their lives. Why not explore how you can serve a higher purpose in life by making a difference for your community today? In my opinion, living a good life means that you interact with the world, and care for yourself and for others. A way to do that would be to help people leading the way, and showing them how to support each other. Because of your experience you understand the importance of relationships. Can you imagine yourself giving the same attention to other people as you used to give to your wife? Think about the chemistry you could create with so many people. Think of what that would mean for your community, for the prosperity of your world and for your legacy. Think of what that would mean to you. Doing good really starts with one small gesture: engage with your environment. Be part of it and add value by simply giving your attention to other people. To be truly present in your world requires being authentic and genuine. Be authentic, which is to tell what you do and do what you tell. Be genuine, which is to be a real person with true feelings and doubts.

The first thing you should do now is to jump out of a plane, with a parachute that is! Make a three-week road trip on your motorbike. Go camping for five days in the middle of nowhere. Swim with the sharks, or climb the K2. Do something that you've been thinking about for a long time, but never got to do. The purpose of this is to realize how much you are alive. It widens your spectrum. Leave your familiar environment for a while. There are too many sad emotions hanging around. You need to get out of there and taste, breathe and smell life. The earth is a beautiful place and you're blessed to be part of it. Then come back home and start your project.

Find your purpose in life. If it means to change jobs, change country, change whatever, just do it. Do it and change the world, but do it consciously! This is the moment! Make a plan, and do something that really excites you. If you think it's too big, break down your plan into small pieces, but do it. It is your job, it's everyone's job, to find his or her purpose and role in life. You have to fulfill your mission. So pack up your mission in a way that works in the real world, your world. Do this carefully and remember that you will only succeed when you do something that you like.

You are at a crossroads. Where do you go? Are you heading toward the light or into the darkness? I think you already know the answer to this question, since you chose to read this book. You took action, and that says enough. Again, it may seem a small thing to pick up a book, but houses have been built after laying the very first stone in the cement, and it all goes from there. You now have the choice to build something as big as you want. Don't think that you have to do "everything" at the same time. Just take one step at a time. Focus on adding value and grow steadily into your projects. Then, many years from now and after numerous successes, when you are at the end of your life and you look back, you will be able to smile at a great legacy.

A DEFINING MOMENT

One summer afternoon I was in New York. I was heading out with my sister and our cousin. I was all set to go and waiting for the two girls to get ready too. While I was standing at the door, it was as if I suddenly felt a kiss on my left cheek. The others didn't notice anything as they were grabbing their stuff, but I was almost certain to have felt this kiss, as if it were a farewell kiss. Somehow I thought of Judith saying goodbye. She had to go on a journey, a voyage that didn't include me. Our roads separated there; I had to go on, on my own. This was my defining moment. I decided there and then, that I would start building a life worth living; a life that Judith would be proud of; but most of all, a life that I would be proud of. I didn't just want to look back in the past anymore. I literally turned myself around, opened up the door and walked out.

Although the road from there on has been quite bumpy and steep, I finally found my way. I discovered what I like to do best. I cannot be more pleased than to help others develop themselves and their lives to their full potential. I want to make everyone aware of the fact that we have to really live our lives, that we have just one that's been given to us. It is our job to fulfill it to the maximum, not just by talking about our dreams and wishes, but also by acting upon them. We have to get out of the stands and we have to go onto the field. We have to state our values and live by them. I know that even if I would touch only one heart in the process, my life has been worthwhile.

RECAP

I hope *The Widowers' Manual* has been some sort of inspiration to you. I hope it has helped you realize that although a part of your life is over, your life in total isn't. Life is still very present, and it has a deeper meaning for you now, a meaning you understand better. A meaning you create or can create. Do this with your life's values; the principles you live by. Maybe they're old values and maybe there are some brand new ones. That doesn't matter. The importance is that they suit you. Live by them truthfully and your days will seem longer as they will be fuller. The energy you need to perform on a top level in life is not going to come to you from some outside source. It comes from within you. You will experience that, as you gain clarity of your goal and the path that you will follow. Don't settle for anything less than doing the thing that you love. You will know it when you find it. Always follow your heart. You understand now how fragile life is and how limited your time can be. Do not waste your life by living someone else's life: live your own. Think for yourself and determine the road toward your dream so you can create your own world with its own specifications. While you do this, act on the Widowers' Manual Anchors I have offered you in this book. They are once again:

Anchor 1 Feel:

Accept that the pain is there. Take notice of it and choose that it's all right to be in pain so it's off your plate. If you don't worry about pain you will have the space and the opportunity to actually start moving toward your new dream.

Don't let the pain get you off track. Keep your eyes on the prize. When you have clarity regarding where to go, you will not be distracted by fear. Fear is usually the reason for people to not take action. If that is the case you will stay where you are and eventually even go backwards.

Use the pain as leverage. Open your eyes and look for alternative routes and then use the pain in order to motivate yourself to actually take the first step in a new direction.

Embrace the pain. Welcome it, and link it to the love you feel for your wife. The more it hurts, the better it is. Laugh at it; get acquainted with it. You will be handling its impact easier in the course of time.

Anchor 2 Share:

Don't hide yourself. Don't think you can manage the loss by yourself. You need others. Besides, in your new world you are going to be highly socially visible. Start now by being the person you want to be.

Stop assuming. You don't know what others think. Ask questions instead.

Position yourself powerfully. Be an inspiring and energetic leader. Pioneer into a new direction in a new world. Have your knowledge and your empathy teamed up.

Choose your words well. The better you phrase your words, the higher the quality of the feedback.

Anchor 3 Dare:

Show your vulnerability. Be brave and be human. You're not Superman, and don't pretend to be him. Dare to lower the wall you've pulled up around you. In this way you can go out, and help can come in.

Learn to receive. You deserve it. It is neither about competence nor a power game. Accept the offered help gladly and say "Thanks".

Have the courage to let go. Walking forward while looking back over your shoulder is not an advisable method to proceed. If it is progress that you want, dare to let go. It will give you peace.

Anchor 4 Meet:

Create a special environment for special people. Introduce your story to new people and especially a new girlfriend with care. When you're ready, introduce her to your family and friends in a subtle way. Give as much attention to people as they need, and take your time.

Share your ups and downs. Be honest and open with the people in your life. If you are going to get involved with someone special again, include her in your life. Communicate on a very detailed level your activities. Assure her of your love for her.

Keep the long-term goal in mind. Other people's rules are not your rules. People are like plants; either they grow or die. There's nothing in the middle, so, continue to move forward into the new direction you have set for yourself.

Anchor 5 Care:

Don't play God. Be humble, don't judge and don't compare your situation to those of others.

Truly respect other people. Let's respect each other. Let's respect what we do, what we think and the way we choose to act in order to grow into a better version of ourselves. Let's appreciate the diversity amongst people. Let's respect each other's reality.

Serve and help others. Contributing to others is both inspiring and compelling. Changing patterns expands your world.

Comprehend that you're worth it. The outcome of your actions depends on the level of your self worth, and this depends highly on the level of your self-acceptance. Show the world the real you.

The world is in turmoil right now. It looks as if it's upside down. However, while honoring one of my values "being positive", I have been thinking about the impact of a strong emotional experience like the death of a spouse. What could it mean for you in a broader perspective in our current society? Where are we, and where do we want to go?

Today's world seems to be one of more awareness, people are more concerned about their way of living and what consequences that lifestyle has on the environment and on the world in general. People are more thoughtful about how they spend their lives.

We feel we have to live our lives now. We have to enjoy our loved ones now. We should ask ourselves significant yet basic questions like, "What about us? What about our life? What about our personal development? How do I get the best and the most out of my life as a professional, as a father, as a friend, as a human being and as a world citizen? What about our children?" Actually think of what world you are going to leave them. Would you want to live in that world? It is time to raise awareness for these questions. It is time to think what happens after we're gone, not just while we're here. Our children look at us when they want to learn new things. We therefore have to be good role models and we have to be great teachers.

Development starts at a very young age. The Dutch word for development is "ontwikkeling" which literally means, "unwrapping". I find the Dutch description appealing, as if you unwrap a mummy's cloth in order to see the actual person inside the package. So maybe we've got it in reverse; maybe we are born with all the answers already packed inside of us. As Michelangelo already saw the statue of David in the rock, he just got rid of the unnecessary pieces of marble, perhaps we just need to unwrap ourselves, as we grow older in order to fully blossom at a later stage. Maybe we have to search for the questions and link them with the existing answers inside of us.

NEW CONSCIOUSNESS

A new consciousness of how to actually "be" is rising. After all, we are human *beings*, not human doings. Why wouldn't we focus on the really important matters in life? You know what those are; they are the metamorphoses of your values. We need to think for ourselves, and we have to take the responsibility for our own well being. Being aware of how to be, comes forth from the knowledge that the time given to us is short; it is scarce. Scarcity normally makes people more thoughtful and active. So let's be considerate and bold. In this regard it is also important to develop a new attitude toward overcoming the death of a partner. The subject could be discussed in a new way. We could teach our world about how we have dealt with death. That it is an end, but not our end. We need to share that we understand the concept of scarcity now better than ever before. We get that this is our time and that we have to act upon our dreams and wishes now. We could show that we are able to do this with all the respect in the world for our deceased wives. We could do this together with our self-respect and respect for life itself. Equally important, we should show that men are able to display and develop their empathetic side.

We have to show that the combination of empathy and practicality goes hand in hand. As a matter of fact, it's a fantastic mix. It adds value to your environment.

GET ON THE ROAD

I challenge you to take up this new role. Start in your own community, and don't let your uncertainty keep you from developing yourself. Follow the anchors together with the values you distinguish for yourself and you will be able to contribute fully to society and grow as a human being. It is in periods of high emotional states that men grow to their full potential. You have had an expensive lesson long before your time. You have the opportunity now to transform this experience as a powerful tool toward a greater future. Just act on it; get on the road, which has opened up for you. Take your trip to a higher level of performance, achievement and morality.

Share your story with the world on what you do to exit what seems a hopelessly destructive phase in your life. Seemingly, because now you know things are not as they seem. They are as you make them. Do that with intensity, passion and energy, so that you will move toward a higher degree of being. Take your journey, you will enjoy it.

Get yourself going with the Widowers' Manual Anchors. It is through the absorption and application of the anchors that you will get better at putting them to use. Stick with it, and understand that it's going to be hard at first, but it will get easier along the way as it doesn't become so consuming. As soon as you get competence you'll get confidence, and you only get confidence if you know what to try and what to do. So practice the anchors, take one step at a time and don't get overwhelmed. I said it before; you don't have to apply all the anchors at the same time. Take your time, and try and master the steps I laid out for you in this book. Already there are many people who are rushing into the things they have to do. These people all want to do everything at the same time, but they are trying to go too fast and that's exactly why a lot of people in the world do not succeed in what they were set out to do. It is all right if you don't get results quickly. All great things in life have been built over time. I know for example that your first attempt to use the pain as leverage is going to be miserable, because you still feel miserable. Yet you have to give it a try anyway, and don't let it discourage you. It's like riding a bicycle; at first you have no clue how to keep balance and how you get the thing to stop other than breaking with your feet, but while you keep on trying you'll get better at it. You improve because you are actually riding the bike. Of course you will fall a couple of times and that will be painful, but that's part of the learning process and it's the reason why you feel satisfied once you get the hang of it.

It's the same thing with practicing the anchors. At first you will find it hard and maybe applying them even seems unnatural to you sometimes. I encourage you however to stick with them. Once you know how to use them to your full benefit, new opportunities will reveal themselves to you. I think you have picked up this book to learn something and so I wanted to give you a push. It is supposed to be hard. The experience of losing your wife has changed your vision of the world dramatically, but the recovery and rebuilding process by utilizing the anchors will change your life forever.

At the end, at *your* end, you want to know whether or not you have made a difference in your life. I encourage you to think about this in terms of the number of worlds you've changed and hearts you have touched. So just go, go and get ready to touch some hearts. Start with the first one: your own. Decide it is all right to move on. Decide that you're worth it. I tell you, that you are.

I salute you here, wishing you wisdom and strength, but above all, I acknowledge you. You are a human being, realizing that in spite of what has happened, you do have choices and possibilities in your life. So choose, live and start today.

Go out there and conquer the world. The door is open.

ACKNOWLEDGEMENTS

To my daughter, Margherita. You have given my life color in a very abundant way. I love you more than words can express.

To my parents, Gert and Marlous, for creating the possibility to write this book. You have stood by me at a close range from the very first beginning, and you have helped me out wherever you could. Mom, dad, I love you. Thank you so much for everything.

To one of my best friends, Carlo Aagten. You are a very dear friend who advised me on numerous occasions in the past, and especially your availability I hold very dear. C, I love you buddy!

Thanks to my friend Professor Karl Herbst. You have helped me enormously with editing this book. I have one word for you, Karl: Wow!

To my family and friends who were at my side fifteen years ago and who have helped me through the years, which followed. Thank you Barbara Looten, Raymond Slotboom, Max Genevace,

Bart Hamelijnck, Evelien Rimmelzwaan, Willem Genevace, and the Wegman family, Marina, Wim, Désirée, Wendy and Bas.

To my friend Marco de Pasquale. Without you I would not have taken the road that I'm on today. Thank you very much!

To the numerous people I did not mention. Although in some cases the contacts have become less frequent in the last years, I will not forget our times together.

Last but certainly not least I want to acknowledge and thank my current wife Olga; you are one of the most beautiful persons and spirits I have ever met in my life. I know how hard it has been for you the last 10 years. This book is about widowers who are having a hard time in getting up and moving along, but I know that it has been extremely tough for you as my new wife living up to so many expectations and dealing with so many rules, which others have tried to imply onto you. I want you to know that if it hadn't been for you, I would have never been able to write this book. You have given me the space to make my mistakes, and you have helped me to create an environment in which I have been able to find my way toward my dream. You have been riding the roller coaster with me for all these years, and although we are sometimes dizzy and nauseous of the ride, we are still inside one of the carts. I know the upcoming track will be smoother, so let's enjoy the ride a little while longer.

You will always be in my heart.

ABOUT THE AUTHOR

 WOUTER LOOTEN is a Motivational Trainer and Life Coach in the field of personal development.

Wouter lost his wife at the age of twenty-nine. In a period of his life where he was concentrating solely on building a future both professionally and privately, he was brutally confronted with a sudden destruction instead.

He learned to use this experience as leverage to achieve for what he feels is important in life and in the years following the death of his wife he therefore decided to dedicate his life helping others to create a compelling future. He wrote *The Widowers' Manual* and he founded his own coaching academy where he helps people who have endured loss to regain clarity, energy and presence so that they effectively and profoundly regenerate toward a great and fulfilling life.

Wouter has held several management positions with large multinational companies prior to his decision to share his knowledge, experience and vision with the world. He is Dutch, but he has lived in several European countries, which has offered him a broad experience of several distinctive cultural heritages. This has highly enlarged his scope and expertise in the field of how to deal with people with different backgrounds, references, lifestyles and views of the world.

Meet him at wouterlooten.com

BUY A SHARE OF THE FUTURE IN YOUR COMMUNITY

These certificates make great holiday, graduation and birthday gifts that can be personalized with the recipient's name. The cost of one S.H.A.R.E. or one square foot is $54.17. The personalized certificate is suitable for framing and will state the number of shares purchased and the amount of each share, as well as the recipient's name. The home that you participate in "building" will last for many years and will continue to grow in value.

Here is a sample SHARE certificate:

HABITAT FOR HUMANITY

THIS CERTIFIES THAT
YOUR NAME HERE
HAS INVESTED IN A HOME FOR A DESERVING FAMILY

1985-2010
TWENTY-FIVE YEARS OF BUILDING FUTURES
IN OUR COMMUNITY ONE HOME AT A TIME

1200 SQUARE FOOT HOUSE @ $65,000 = $54.17 PER SQUARE FOOT
This certificate represents a tax deductible donation. It has no cash value.

YES, I WOULD LIKE TO HELP!

I support the work that Habitat for Humanity does and I want to be part of the excitement! As a donor, I will receive periodic updates on your construction activities but, more importantly, I know my gift will help a family in our community realize the dream of homeownership. **I would like to SHARE in your efforts against substandard housing in my community!** *(Please print below)*

PLEASE SEND ME _____ SHARES at $54.17 EACH = $ $_____

In Honor Of: _____

Occasion: (Circle One)   HOLIDAY   BIRTHDAY   ANNIVERSARY

     OTHER: _____

Address of Recipient: _____

Gift From: _____ *Donor Address:* _____

Donor Email: _____

I AM ENCLOSING A CHECK FOR $ $_____ PAYABLE TO HABITAT FOR HUMANITY OR PLEASE CHARGE MY VISA OR MASTERCARD *(CIRCLE ONE)*

Card Number _____ Expiration Date: _____

Name as it appears on Credit Card _____ Charge Amount $ _____

Signature _____

Billing Address _____

Telephone # Day _____ Eve _____

PLEASE NOTE: Your contribution is tax-deductible to the fullest extent allowed by law.
Habitat for Humanity • P.O. Box 1443 • Newport News, VA 23601 • 757-596-5553
www.HelpHabitatforHumanity.org

9 781614 481805